OSI·720

fig·50

GW00493537

# QUALITY CIRCLES
A practical guide

To Bee

# QUALITY CIRCLES
## A practical guide

MIKE ROBSON

Gower

Published by
Gower Publishing Company Limited
Aldershot, Hants, England
Reprinted 1983, 1984, 1985

British Library Cataloguing in Publication Data

Robson, Mike
   Quality circles.
   1. Quality control
   I. Title
   658.5'62    TS156

   ISBN 0-566-02343-1

Typeset by Pintail Studios Ltd,
Ringwood, Hampshire
Printed and bound in Great Britain by
Biddles Ltd, Guildford and King's Lynn

# CONTENTS

# CONTENTS

# PREFACE

I have been involved with Quality Circles for some three years now and, with each week that has passed, my commitment has increased. The more I talked with people about it, and helped companies to introduce programmes, the clearer it has become to me that the Quality Circles concept is a complex and sensitive instrument. If applied simplistically it will not fulfil its potential. More dangerous than this is the possibility that programmes will be introduced under the Quality Circles label which are not truly Quality Circles. I hope that my book will help to avoid this danger.

The book introduces and explains the Quality Circles concept. It goes on to outline an implementation programme and to indicate the training inputs needed for co-ordinators, Circle helpers and Circle leaders. To that extent the book stands on its own. Once a decision is made to proceed, however, it becomes an integral part of the Gower Quality Circles programme.

The second part of this programme consists of a training package comprising three main elements. Firstly there are four audio tapes containing the eight pre-recorded training sessions. The running time of each tape varies, depending on the subject, from fifteen to thirty minutes. Secondly, there is a training manual containing recommended lesson plans for the Circle leader to use in conducting each session. Not all Circle leaders will be experienced trainers, and for that reason the manual includes not only a complete transcript of the audio material but also guidance as to when to stop the tape to review progress, when to change visual aids, and suggested questions to ask at various points. Thirdly, there are master copies of nearly 200 specially designed visual aids. Their cartoon-style approach introduces a lighthearted touch, but each one drives home an important teaching point. The masters can be used to create, as required, overhead transparencies, 35 mm slides, or flip charts.

Thus the training package represents a complete system for teaching the techniques required for an effective Quality Circle. The eight topics covered are:

An introduction to Quality Circles
Problem solving
Brainstorming
Analysing problems
Collecting data
Presenting to management
Working together
Dealing with problems in the group

The third main item in the programme is a members' handbook, supplied in sets of ten so that a copy can be given to everyone involved. The handbook explains the Quality Circle concept and principles and contains the transcripts of the audio tapes, illustrated by the visual aids used in the training sessions. This handbook is important in a number of ways. Firstly, it relieves Circle members from all pressure to memorise the problem-solving techniques as they are being trained. Since members each have a copy of the book, they are able to study any subject as often as they wish. Furthermore it dispenses with the need to take notes during the training session. The ability to follow the taped lesson in the book reduces the feeling of threat often associated with learning new skills. Finally, the handbook serves as a formal statement of training received. The certificates which are supplied as part of the complete programme also fulfil this role, but many Circle members will regard their own copy of the handbook as an equally important record.

Now how is all this material likely to be used? Companies who have already decided to use Quality Circles will want to acquire the complete programme, since it gives them the tools they need to do the job. For companies who wish to know more about the concept, the present book contains enough information to enable them to decide whether or not to go ahead and what additional help they might need. Once the decision is made, this 'practical guide' performs a further vital role in defining the programme of introduction and in the actual training of the co-ordinator, the facilitator(s) – who are the Circle helpers – and the Circle leaders. The training package will also be required for these tasks. Having been used in the training of these people, this package is available for use by Circle leaders, supported by the facilitators, in the training of Circle members. A copy of the members' handbook is given to the co-ordinator, facilitators and Circle leaders, and then to each Circle member. The members' copies should be handed out at the beginning, not only so that they can be used in the training sessions, but also as a token of management commitment. The Quality Circles approach will not work to maximum effect if it is adopted piecemeal. It requires careful planning, a substantial amount of training and no little skill. This programme provides a framework for any company wishing to introduce the concept.

Here and there in this book I refer to the related materials. These references are of course for the benefit of those using the complete programme and may safely be ignored by readers who have only the book itself. For the sake of simplicity I have used the pronoun 'he' to stand for 'he or she'. All of the roles in Quality Circles can be filled expertly by members of either sex.

My main hopes for this book are twofold. Firstly, that it will help companies to choose whether or not to introduce Quality Circles. Secondly, that, if they decide to go ahead, it will – in combination with the other materials in the Gower programme – enable them to do so with a full understanding of what is involved.

Finally, I should like to express my gratitude to Wayne and Roma Rieker, who first introduced me to the Quality Circles approach. It is their pioneering more than anything else that has helped to spread both the concept and practice throughout North America and Europe, and everyone in the Quality Circle movement owes them an immense debt.

Mike Robson

**Part I**
# THE QUALITY CIRCLES CONCEPT

# Chapter 1

# INTRODUCTION

A Quality Circle is a group of four to ten volunteers working for the same supervisor or foreman who meet once a week, for an hour, under the leadership of the supervisor, to identify, analyse and solve their own work-related problems. Beneath the apparent simplicity of this definition lies a concept, and an approach to a range of organisational problems, of remarkable sophistication and power.

Quality Circles have proved successful in all continents of the world, across the whole range of industries and in every function of a business, from Sales to Production, from Accounts to Engineering. The only administrative pre-requisite for setting up a Quality Circle programme is that there are enough people working for any one supervisor or foreman who want to operate it. The consideration of working for the same person is waived by many who know no better and even some who should. For a programme to be successful in anything but the short term, however, a good deal of knowledge, expertise and resource is required, and this is provided by the set of materials of which this book is the first item.

For many, a Quality Circle represents one more in a long line of management gimmicks which have their day and then fade quickly and quietly into obscurity. Such people will either choose not to use it, or will introduce it to their companies as a 'flavour of the month'. If the idea is introduced in this way, there is no doubt that the Quality Circles *will* be a 'flavour of the month', and will not last. It is worth establishing at the outset that this says little about the approach itself but a lot about the companies that use it in this way.

If Quality Circles are to fulfil their true potential, they need to be introduced and managed with care and understanding of their real nature. At their most general, Quality Circles can help to change the culture of an organisation to one where there is a common ownership of corporate goals, widespread commitment of the workforce, and genuine two-way communication, and where the abilities of all staff are given a real opportunity to develop to high levels of effectiveness, and there is a noticeable improvement in operating performance and company results. Having said this, we must quickly establish that Quality Circles are *not* a panacea or a magic wand. They do not even attempt to be so. The approach is a tool which organisations can use if they choose to, and, as with every other tool, the results achieved will depend upon the knowledge, skill and experience of those using it.

For many companies the approach forms a significant part of their management philosophy from the outset. For others it grows in importance as the full implications and potential become clear. For yet others, as we have already indicated, it will be used as a short-term gimmick. It is unfortunate but inevitable that this will be so. It is only to be hoped, where this is the case, that it is clear to all concerned, and that the approach itself is not blamed after the inevitable demise of such programmes. The philosophy upon which Quality Circles are based is that, given the right conditions, many people in organisations will choose to use more of their abilities and experience to take part in solving work problems. The philosophy is otherwise known as Douglas McGregor's Theory Y, and Quality Circles are the ideal mechanism for making the series of assumptions that comprise Theory Y an operating reality.

In this book we explore in depth three main questions:

firstly, what are Quality Circles all about; secondly, how to introduce a successful Quality Circles programme; and finally, the likelihood of such a programme being successful for you.

## Quality Circles and other techniques

The last few decades have seen many management techniques come, and, for the most part, go. Given this background, it would not be surprising for many people to see Quality Circles in the same light, without first looking at the approach carefully. In fact, substantial differences separate Quality Circles from previous techniques, and it will be useful to look at several other methods to establish why they did not stand the test of time.

During the 1960s management by objectives, advocated and popularised by such eminent people as Odiorne and Humble, caught the imagination of managements up and down the land and, at the time, was widely hailed as the answer to everything; and yet if one asks an average manager who lived through that period what he thinks of management by objectives he is more than likely to snort and dismiss it as another of those gimmicks that fizzled out after six months. So what went wrong? If we consider the concept of management by objectives carefully, we find it says that responsible managers should be treated as such, and should therefore play a very full part in establishing what their goals will be over the next period of time, and, having agreed those key result areas, should go away and do what they said they would do. This process should be followed up with a review to consider the managers' success or lack of it at achieving the agreed objectives, and to begin another round of goal-setting. It is extremely difficult to fault either the philosophy underlying the approach or the logic of it, and yet it usually failed. Why?

There were three main problems associated with the

implementation of management by objectives in practice, and none have anything to do with the concept, which actually remains as sound as ever. The first problem was that it was usually introduced into companies wholesale – 'As of Monday next we are going to have management by objectives'. This was tantamount to saying that the company was now going to become 'management by objectives shaped'. In the light of the average human being's reaction to change, let alone enforced change, it is hardly surprising that the average manager was less than ecstatic about the idea. Therefore, as soon as possible, and by virtue of delicate neglect, things 'got back to normal'.

The second main cause of the failure of management by objectives was that, in the way it was introduced into the majority of companies, it quickly became tangled up in bureaucracy. In so many cases it was a veritable paper-producing machine, and there is nothing more infuriating to the average manager, supervisor or member of staff than an over-abundance of 'useless' paper. Inevitably forms were filled in late, even in retrospect nobody read the contents, and the whole process became divorced from the real world. This process of tying the concept into a formal paperwork system gives the clue to the third main reason for the demise of the approach.

Management by objectives at its purest does not need form-filling, with copies sent to all and sundry. Real management by objectives is about achieving Douglas McGregor's Theory Y with managers, and can be done on the back of an envelope as far as paperwork is concerned. The problem here was that many of the companies that introduced the concept did so in a Theory X way, presumably because they, or their advisers, believed in that theory. Why else was there felt to be such a requirement for outside control?

It is no real surprise, then, in view of these three reasons, that the concept quickly expired in so many places. But how is the Quality Circles concept different? Firstly, Quality Circles do not try to make the organisation 'Quality Circle shaped'. An abiding principle of the approach is that any programme starts in a very small way, and only grows at the pace dictated by employees wanting to join in. Consequently, it puts no reactive pressure on people's tolerance for change.

Secondly, Quality Circles are as unbureaucratic as possible. The only piece of paper required is an 'action minutes' statement after each meeting, which is needed for good communications, to ensure that all interested parties are kept informed of progress in the groups.

Thirdly, Quality Circles are voluntary. They give people in the business the opportunity of using more of their talents at work if they so desire, and assume they have the capability and also the ability to make their own choices. Quality Circles are about the practical application of so-called Theory Y.

Job enrichment enjoyed something of a vogue in the 1960s and 1970s. Based on the work of Professor Herzberg, who in turn was heavily influenced by Maslow, it laid down that motivation at work arose from people being able to satisfy their higher-level needs. Maslow's hierarchy of needs states that there are five levels of need felt by humans: basic needs such as air, water, food and so on, security needs, social needs, self-esteem needs, and finally needs for self-actualisation. The basis of the theory is that only unsatisfied needs act as motivators and that, once a person has more or less satisfied his needs at one level, the next level of unsatisfied needs will 'reveal' itself to him and motivate him to attempt to fulfil it. Herzberg's research led him to believe that the pressing unsatisfied needs among people at work were the higher-level needs of self-esteem and self-actualisation, and that programmes of job enrichment were required to motivate people to try to fulfil these needs.

Some very careful work was done by many companies

7

in structuring job-enrichment programmes, but many of the attempts did not really get off the ground. Again this was probably less to do with the concept itself than the fact that such exercises were almost invariably seen by the workforce as management initiatives. It could be argued, of course, that the Quality Circle approach is also a management initiative, but there is one crucial difference. Quality Circles are owned by the members. This is a clear and specific part of the approach, whereas with job-enrichment programmes the ownership was often felt by the workforce to have remained with management. Without this transfer of ownership any programme is unlikely to succeed in the long term.

Transactional analysis was another technique used by many companies in an attempt to improve the quality of management and supervision through a greater understanding of the nature of relationships. Transactional Analysis, or TA as it is more usually known, is a very powerful tool for evaluating the real nature of relationships, and indeed is relevant to the understanding of Quality Circles. Again, however, attempts to make TA the basis of a 'brave new world' were generally unsuccessful, this time because TA, useful though it is as a guide to human relations, does not give participants enough 'real world' problem-solving activity to be successful as a total strategy in its own right.

Quality Circles, then, are substantially different from previous approaches in that the ownership is vested differently, they are not 'paper-generating machines', they do not attempt to change things overnight, and, maybe most important of all, they are intensely practical. This is why people join them. They get things done.

## The deceptive simplicity of Quality Circles

It is possible, of course, to take a much more simplistic view of Quality Circles. Some people explain the approach as being simply a matter of getting groups of workers together and giving them some problems to talk about!

Indeed, one of the problems with the Quality Circle approach is that it sounds simple. In fact, it is not at all easy when applied properly, as is instanced by one major company, which stated that it had taken it five years to get to the point where it understood the concept and where the concept was working optimally. Perhaps not everyone would take as long as that, but there is a point here that can seriously affect the longer-term development of a programme in any company. Put bluntly, if Quality Circles are introduced and treated in a simplistic manner, they are unlikely to last for very long; they are more likely to fizzle out as other techniques in the past have done.

What, therefore, constitutes the complexity of the approach? Basically it is to do with people, their perceptions, reactions and motivations. Quality Circles assume that the average working person has a brain as well as a pair of hands, and the approach is a mechanism for enabling and encouraging employees to use their undoubted abilities to solve their own problems at work and thereby make their jobs more interesting and less frustrating. It does this in many companies, however, in a climate of 'us and them', low trust and a high level of scepticism among managers and employees alike. In such a minefield both skill and care are needed. The principles on which Quality Circles are based can help to improve 'the way things are done round here' for the benefit of all, but only if the broader implications of the approach are understood.

## The vital role of management
The importance of middle-management backing for the programme cannot be overstressed (see Chapter 10). The need to develop management commitment, however, has often to be viewed against the background of prevailing frustration and cynicism. Quality Circles are not a

panacea and do not try to be. The approach has no magic wand that will suddenly make everyone positive-minded and committed, but then neither has anything else! What Quality Circles can do is to provide a framework for the development of more productive attitudes and relationships between different levels of the business. The gestation period will be variable, and will depend on a number of factors, including the prevailing attitudes and the personal views of individuals. One thing is certain: changes of any depth and meaning are not likely overnight.

The Quality Circle approach has much to offer management, of that there is no doubt, and this topic is covered more fully in Chapter 10, which concentrates attention on the subject, but one general point is worth making at the outset. One of the keys to effectiveness is resource management. For a manager the resources he controls can be viewed as being goods and services, people and money. A key to the effective use of the people resource is to employ its abilities in achieving the goals of the organisation and its members. An important part of this is to solve problems in the right place – where the problems occur. Here Quality Circles can be of the greatest benefit to management and the company, as well as those who choose to take part at Circle level. The fact is that many managers, in environments where there are no Quality Circles, find themselves having to spend far too much time for their liking getting to grips with problems which have nothing to do with them, problems which are really the supervisors' or staff's. What Quality Circles can do, and do effectively, is to change this, by encouraging supervisors and staff to solve their own problems in an organised and professional manner, which in its own turn gives management more time to deal with issues that do need to be dealt with at management's level.

It can be seen, therefore, that the criticism some people level at the approach, which is that Circles only do what would have been done anyway, is only half true. Certainly some of the projects that Circles work on would have been tackled by management, but the point is that this could only have happened at the expense of tackling a different problem. The problem with time is that it is a non-renewable resource: if it is spent on one thing, it cannot be spent on another. One benefit that Quality Circles offer the manager, therefore, is the opportunity to get more done in the department through utilising more of the inherent abilities of the people in it. This can only be accomplished if there is a structure to work within, and appropriate training is given to those who are being encouraged to take on the problem-solving role. Quality Circles for the manager are a very practical, time-freeing mechanism, therefore, as well as being a means of expressing a philosophy of management that recognises the intrinsic abilities of people in general.

## Quality Circles and the trade unions

A question that is always raised early in any discussion about Quality Circles concerns the reaction of the trade unions to the approach. In fact, the great majority of stewards and convenors express a belief in the principles underlying Quality Circles, and this view has been substantiated by research indicating that virtually all shop stewards are in favour of participation if the right mechanism can be found. If there are worries, they are worries about the motives of management. No one likes to feel manipulated, and it is understandable that people will want to find out whether the company views Quality Circles as a short-term gimmick or as a long-term part of the way the company is run. This underlines the need for clear goals and good communications in introducing Quality Circles, and strengthens the case against introducing the concept simply to be fashionable. It will not succeed for long under those circumstances, and will not deserve the willingness, commitment and effort of staff either.

The trade unions' view seems to be that Quality Circles are philosophically sound, and can be utilised as a means for improvement, but only if the motivations of companies in introducing them are 'pure'. Purity in this respect can include the motivation of cost effectiveness, along with those of real opportunity for participation of the workforce, development of higher levels of genuine satisfaction at work, genuinely effective two-way communications, and people development.

Quality Circles do not supplant or threaten unions. Circles are precluded from working on problems which are already and naturally the prerogative of other bodies to solve, and jointly negotiated issues come firmly within this category. Perhaps the most eloquent statement about union reaction to Circles is that the majority of stewards, given the opportunity to join a Circle, do so. Introduced with care and for the right reasons, Quality Circles will fulfil their potential in any company. This potential affects everyone in the company, for Quality Circles are about everyone winning, whether or not everyone does, or wants to, play an active part.

### But it won't work here!
There is sometimes a temptation to see so many of the complexities and problems of a new idea that these swamp the potential advantages being offered. This can happen with Quality Circles, as with any change. It is important, therefore, to establish that the approach has worked in the most difficult circumstances: situations where, for example, the shift system has been so complex that the people working it did not understand how it operated! It works in process industries, engineering works, service industries, offices, banks, workshops and on the factory floor. Industries with very difficult industrial relations have introduced the concept

successfully, and are making it work. It requires effort, commitment and the allocation of the required resources to start up and support the programme. Given these, it can succeed.

Of course, in the beginning much requires to be taken on trust. A further safeguard, therefore, is that Circle programmes should always be started on a pilot basis. Starting small is a vital ingredient of long-term success, since it enables the approach to be tailored to the particular needs of the company. It also enables any organisation to check the feasibility of the concept in its environment without committing an inordinate amount of time and resources to it in the early stages. Given this principle, any company can legitimately conduct a pilot scheme for six months or so before finally deciding whether or not to expand its programme.

**Typical benefits**

There are two distinct and important sets of benefits which accrue from Quality Circles programmes. Firstly, and many would say most importantly, there is a range of usually non-quantifiable results to do with the general attitudes of people at all levels in the organisation. The development of more productive attitudes does not happen instantly; it is a process which takes time, often a long time. Equally, it is a process which does not affect everyone: there will always be those who, for one reason or another, see Circles in a negative light. A remarkable feature of the approach, however, is the proportion of people who do become advocates and devotees.

Many Circle members view their own development in terms of new knowledge. A typical comment from a Circle member is, 'I've been in the company for thirty years and I've learned more in the last six months since becoming a Quality Circle member than I did in my previous twenty-nine years'. Supervisors also often see the development of more productive attitudes in their work groups as a result of Circles. A comment made by one leader gives the flavour: 'Since we have started Quality Circles my lads talk about Circle business in their breaks rather than football and how much beer they drank last night.' The response of management to the changes they see in staff is invariably very positive, as is shown by such comments as, 'It is not so much the solution that is so impressive, it's the way they went about tackling the problem'. Other, previously sceptical, managers often say, 'I'm amazed, I really didn't think they had it in them'. Staff previously difficult to manage are frequently those in whom the greatest change is seen. Very often the former attitude of such people is born of frustration and boredom, and Quality Circles give them something to get their teeth into. One Circle leader said, 'I wouldn't have picked one member, but as he volunteered I was stuck with him. His attitude has changed now; he talks to me. He never did before!'

Changes are also seen in Circle leaders. Members make such comments as, 'It's much easier to respect him now', 'We could never talk to him before but now we have a really good relationship', and, 'He's a much better supervisor now than he was before'. Circle leaders see the development in themselves very clearly. One group of four supervisors wrote an entirely unsolicited report which focused on the need to expand the programme and detailed the steps made in their own development as major reasons for broadening the base. The benefits they saw themselves gaining were in both confidence and competence – confidence in stand-up roles, such as teaching the members and presenting to managers, and in the general task of leadership; and competence in problem-solving and in effective and appropriate man management. Management see the improvements in performance or supervision just as clearly, and point to better communications as a major benefit. Even managers who were understandably sceptical at the beginning very often become converted by the work that is done by the

Circle and by the sometimes quite dramatic improvement in performance from the supervisors who choose to take part.

When Circle members review the changes in attitude that they perceive among managers, they point mainly to significant improvements in communication. This, they claim, leads to a greater and more obvious commitment to making things better, rather than simply protecting the status quo. The ability to talk to management in a meaningful way, assumed to be lacking before, is a major change in the eyes of Circle members, and it is no good saying that the opportunity is always available, for if it is not perceived to be there, then for all practical purposes it is not. Supervisors, again, look to improved communications as the most significant change in relation to their managers; the willingness to listen is often cited as a key point at this level. Managers themselves usually perceive that their departments run more smoothly as a result of the approach, and that they have more time to spend on dealing with their own work, instead of constantly having to sort out other people's difficulties. This is not to say, of course, that Quality Circles make a manager's job easier – in many ways it is the opposite – but any increase in difficulty is invariably of the positive kind. It is a pressure to manage everyone's attempts to improve performance throughout, rather than the awful difficulty associated with just keeping things going by oneself. Loath though we may be to admit it, many perfectly capable managers are much nearer to the latter situation than the former. Quality Circles can help, by giving people a framework within which they can encourage improvements. They are not a magic wand, as we have said before, but if handled correctly they can be an enormously powerful tool.

Changes in attitudes at all levels are one of the important non-quantifiable benefits that accrue to companies who embark on Quality Circle programmes, but there are others, significant among which is the spreading of a problem-solving ethic throughout the whole organisation. In many businesses a measure of problem avoidance is usually achieved through pointing fingers at other people and departments, but Quality Circles do much to confront the problem and encourage people at all levels to commit themselves to making improvements rather than merely protecting the status quo. This feeling of participation in, and commitment to, the process of improving the performance of the company is a vital part of the health of any organisation.

The development of supervisory performance is a further important benefit that invariably accompanies Quality Circles programmes; indeed, some companies have decided to go ahead with their introduction primarily to achieve this benefit. Interestingly and importantly the power of the approach in developing supervision is seen at all levels in the organisation, from the subordinates of those in question right up to senior management, and including the supervisors themselves.

The improvements tend, first, to be in the area of man management and communication. Many Circle members note the improvement in both the quality and the quantity of communication as a result of starting a group in the section. The approach really does encourage two-way communication, and is one of the very few mechanisms available that can genuinely claim this. Briefing groups, for example, useful though they may be, are essentially one-way communication devices. Development in the more general man-management aspects of supervision occurs progressively as the supervisor understands more about the motivations and expectations of his people, and as the, often unspoken, barriers are confronted and the difficulties talked about and resolved. The second area of supervisory development is in the practical skill of organised problem-solving. Supervisors utilise the training they are given to solve problems inside and outside the Circle. The third area of

16

benefit lies in the fact that Quality Circles put the supervisors in a leadership role within the group.

It is a very widely held perception that the role of the supervisor has been seriously diminished during the past years, in many businesses to the point that he is little more than a progress-chaser. Furthermore, he has often lost his identity and does not know where to position himself. He is, in many cases, like the nut in the nutcrackers. Attempts have been made through myriad training courses to teach supervisors the 'classical' rudiments of their trade, but many such courses, though often of high technical merit, have failed to survive the jump back to the real and difficult world outside the classroom. Quality Circles have a huge advantage here, in that the 'bridge' is ready-made. Furthermore, because of the availability of help in the early stages of Circle formation and development, Circle leaders can flex their problem-solving and group-development muscles in reasonable safety. The entirely practical nature of the approach is seen by members and leaders alike as a tremendous benefit, and certainly for supervisors this feature is the real catalyst to the development of their skills and their perception of their role, not only during the work of the Circle but during the rest of the week as well.

Changes in attitude, the advancement of a problem-solving ethic, and the development of supervisory performance are significant, but probably the most important of the range of non-quantifiable benefits is the power of Quality Circles as a method of promoting, and achieving, the genuine participation of a much wider range of staff than has been achieved by other methods. This is not to say that this approach should replace anything that is being done at present; indeed, one of the great attractions of Quality Circles is that in many ways it taps fertile new ground. Quality Circles should and do fit in with any systems of representation, consultation and communications that are currently in operation in the company, whether they be a framework of management and union negotiation, consultative committees, briefing groups or any of the many other mechanisms used.

As far as quantifiable benefits are concerned, Quality Circles have demonstrated their cost effectiveness wherever they have been introduced. The world-wide average is a payback of between £5 and £8 for every £1 invested in the programme, and some companies have claimed ratios of benefit to cost of up to 15:1. Of course, a huge range of projects is tackled by Circles, which means that the range of results is also vast. At one end of the spectrum Circles occasionally save huge sums of money. One clerical group devised a solution to a problem of over-delivery of supplies and saved over £300,000 per annum. A production group solved a bottleneck in the testing of a much needed product and generated over £400,000 per annum additional income. A Circle in the shipbuilding industry solved a problem of stores organisation and saved nearly £150,000 per annum. Such examples happen from time to time, but it would be misleading to say that they were an everyday occurrence. At the other end of the spectrum there are solutions put forward by Circles which save a few hundred pounds a year. These are, in fact, very worthwhile, especially when it is realised that a Circle may be solving three or maybe six problems during any year, and that there are a number of Circles generating the tangible results. As might be expected, however, most of the solutions that Circles propose fall somewhere in the middle as far as benefits are concerned, and generate savings of between £1,000 and £10,000. The important point to recognise here is that with Circles solving a number of problems during any year, savings can very quickly add up to a substantial amount.

Finally, as far as benefits are concerned, we need to cover the benefits Circle members feel they get out of the approach. Firstly, there is the ability to influence matters that affect them. This is widely recognised as a key component of motivation at work, a fact with which many Circle members seem to concur. Secondly, the opportunity to get to grips with some of the problems that have been frustrating them, often for years, is cited by many as a key benefit. Often in the past people have felt that they would be either unable to tackle the difficulty or that, quite simply, it was 'not their place'. Circles give the opportunity, and the tools, to do the job.

With Circles, therefore, there is a very wide range of different types of benefit. Various companies and groups will obviously focus on different aspects, according to their interest and need. But it is clear from all the experience that has been gathered over the world that there are benefits for everyone, whatever their position or situation, and that Quality Circles can help materially to improve the culture of an organisation in terms of the way things are done and the assumptions which are made about people and their potential.

## Further reading

Berne, Eric, *Games People Play: The Psychology of Human Relationships*, Grove Press, Inc., 1964; Penguin Books, 1968.

Herzberg, F., *Work and the Nature of Man*, World Publishing Co., New York, 1966.

Humble, John W., *Improving Business Results*, McGraw-Hill, Maidenhead, 1968.

Maslow, A., *Motivation and Personality*, Harper and Row, New York, 1970.

Odiorne, G. S., *Management Decisions by Objectives*, Prentice-Hall, New York, 1961.

# Chapter 2

# DEVELOPMENT OF QUALITY CIRCLES*

Probably the most important point about the history of Quality Circles is that there is one, stretching back to 1962. This separates the movement from many other techniques which have quickly faded away and have not achieved àny widespread application. Quality Circles are not only still around and healthy, but growing at an enormous rate, even in their country of origin, Japan. Before we trace the history of the Quality Circle movement itself, however, it will be useful to explore the circumstances that led up to the development of the approach.

In the late nineteenth century Frederick W. Taylor developed a way of running organisations which had, and still has, a huge impact on the way work is done, the way people are treated, and the assumptions that are made about them by their organisations. Taylor's system, often referred to as Scientific Management, was based on a number of premises, including the following: firstly, there was always one right way to perform a task, and it should be the job of specialist industrial engineers to plan work methods and standards down to the last detail; secondly, workers worked for economic reward and nothing else, and, therefore, differential piecework schemes which rewarded effort should be the basis of

*This chapter contains material from *The Human Side of Enterprise* by Douglas McGregor. Copyright © 1960, Douglas McGregor. Used with the permission of McGraw-Hill Book Company.

payment; and, thirdly, in terms of organisation, line and functional specialisation was optimal.

The Taylor system was often instrumental in achieving substantial increases in productivity, in the short-term at least, and spread like wildfire, becoming the prevailing method of organising work throughout the developed world. During the 1920s, however, an alternative way of doing things, based on achieving high levels of human motivation, began to gain some limited acceptance. Over the subsequent twenty-five years the Human Relations movement, with names like Mayo and Maslow at the forefront, ranged itself against Taylor's Scientific Management, and a great debate started as to which way was most likely to produce positive results.

All this went on in the West against the background of a Japan which had a firmly fixed reputation for producing cheap, shoddy, imitation goods. It was the junk producer of the world.

After the Second World War, however, there was pressure on the Japanese to introduce formal quality control to improve their products, and for the next few years there was a great increase in the number of Japanese businesses using Statistical Quality Control. This programme was spearheaded by an eminent American quality control expert, Dr W. E. Deming. He and a number of other American specialists developed training courses in SQC and helped Japanese industry to introduce the system. SQC, in that it vests responsibility for quality with a number of quality control specialists in a separate department, is a product of Scientific Management. During this period a group was organised in Japan to promote quality control activity in industry. The body was called JUSE, the Japanese Union of Scientists and Engineers, and it still exists today. SQC was a huge success in Japan, helping quality but also productivity, and therefore profitability. Japan was developing quickly and in all respects, including education, where compulsory school attendance was beginning to change the ordinary working man into someone who could not only read and write but who had higher aspirations and expectations than before.

Successful though SQC was in many ways, there were problems; it was not a panacea. Indeed, one of the serious difficulties was that there was a widespread belief that it was. Furthermore, the ownership of the need for quality tended to be vested only in the quality control department and in other interested specialists; there was no widespread commitment either from top management or the workforce at large. Then, in 1954, another eminent American quality specialist went to Japan on a lecture tour. During his visit Dr J. M. Juran introduced a concept that was to have a huge impact on the future development of Japanese industry. The idea was that it was only really feasible to look at quality control in the context of the general managerial task. The implications of this were that the responsibility for the quality of the products made lay with the line and not with a department of quality 'policemen'. The specialist department had a key role in assisting the process, but the ownership of any quality drive had to be vested in line management.

In Japan this message was avidly received and developed into a Japanese version of what is normally known as Total Quality Control. In Japan TQC meant every employee in the organisation having a responsibility for quality, and this, of course, meant that a massive education job needed to be done. Remarkably, one of the ways this was tackled was by a series of radio programmes, aimed mainly at first line supervision, which provided a framework of quality control knowledge. Other activities included prizes, a national quality month, and the awarding of flags and other symbols to mark any company's achievement of quality excellence. Although, possibly, the radio programmes seem a rather 'way-out' idea, it is interesting to note that all the other mechanisms are also used in Western countries.

The last link in the chain leading to Quality Circles was the recognition by at least some of Japan's leading industrialists that the Taylor system was inappropriate as a way of managing an increasingly literate workforce whose aspirations and expectations, depending on how the force was treated, could be directed either towards the achievement of company goals or away from them. In the industrialists' eyes it was necessary to encourage the working man to use his brains as well as his hands, otherwise he would quickly become alienated from both the process and place of work.

The birth of Quality Circles came as a natural development from so-called book-reading circles, which was a suggestion made by Dr K. Ishikawa in the magazine *Quality Control for the Foreman*. These book-reading groups soon began to want to engage in more than theoretical study, and so become problem-solving groups. From here individual foremen encouraged their staff to join in, and Quality Circles were born. This was evolution not revolution, and forms an important part of the approach today. Quality Circles do not try to change the world overnight.

From this small beginning, Quality Circles grew in Japan very slowly at first, but then with increasing speed. By the mid-1970s there were 75,000 Circles registered with JUSE, but it was estimated that there were probably ten times that many who had not formally registered. Over seven million people, therefore, were participating in the movement by that stage.

Earlier, in 1968, a group of Japanese had visited America to expound the benefits of the Quality Circles approach, but had not made significant progress for three main reasons. Firstly, Americans were concerned about the possibility of the approach being culturally based; secondly, the trip happened at a time when many people in America were convinced that their own so-called Zero Defects approach was as effective; and, thirdly because the Japanese team was talking to many people who had been brought up in, and were still committed to, the Taylor system of organising work, with its low expectations of the potential of people at large to do anything but use their muscles and jump at the carrot of economic reward.

In 1973, however, the Lockheed Missiles and Space Company of California sent a team across to look at the concept and found it appealing. The team concluded that Quality Circles were not culturally based – indeed that it was vital to retain as much of the Japanese model as possible if it were to be introduced into the Lockheed Company. The programme introduced into Lockheed was successful, and formed a bridgehead for the launch of the approach in such other American companies as Westinghouse, Harley Davidson, General Motors and Babcock and Wilcox. Progress followed the Japanese experience of slow initial growth leading into increasing activity, as knowledge and experience of the technique became more widely spread, and currently the rate of growth is extremely fast.

In the UK there was scepticism at first, not only of something that had originated in Japan, but also because it had been imported from America. British management was understandably wary. A few companies took the plunge, however, from about 1977 onwards, including ITT and Rolls–Royce. Again a pattern of slow initial development emerged. This was followed by a tremendous explosion of interest, fuelled by articles and reports in a wide range of papers, which led to an increasing number of companies starting Quality Circle programmes. This trend shows no signs of abating; indeed it is rapidly increasing in speed. As one managing director of a company which has had a successful programme for over two years said, 'The question is, can we afford *not* to have them?'

Quality Circles, by 1980, had become a genuinely world-wide movement, with companies from every continent firmly committed to the approach. There are successful programmes in countries as diverse as Korea, Sweden, Taiwan, Brazil, Australia and China, and there is widespread interest, and the beginnings of a movement, in such others as Germany, France, Italy and Spain. The history of Quality Circles then is a history of success. This is not to say, however, that there have not been setbacks and failures. Since it is often possible to learn as much, if not more, from these experiences as from success, it is important that they are considered as part of the history of the movement.

There are three main reasons why a Quality Circles programme might fail. The first concerns the level of resource allocated to the programme. There is little doubt that Quality Circles are sensitive to both the quantity and quality of back-up resource given to them in the early stages. It is vital that there is an acceptance by both the company and the people who will be assisting the development of the programme that an investment of time is required, and that this is crucial to long-term success. The important roles are those of co-ordinator and facilitator. These are dealt with in Chapters 8 and 9, but basically the co-ordinator, who should ideally be a senior manager, is responsible for the development of the programme. The facilitator's role is that of Circle helper in the early stages of any Circle's existence. This task is not easy, and individual Circles and indeed whole programmes have foundered as a result of inappropriate facilitation. The main potential dangers here are, firstly, that the potential facilitators are not trained; since the role of facilitator is not one which is seen particularly often in the normal running of a business, training is clearly required in both understanding the task and developing the skills to be able to cope with it. The second danger is that facilitators may act as technical advisers, thus taking much of the ownership away from the Circle leader and members, and building a dependence on themselves. This is in direct contrast to the role as it should be fulfilled, which is that of developing the group to a stage of self-sufficiency as quickly as is reasonably possible. The third danger is that facilitators may not give the programme the time and overt commitment that it needs. As a rule of thumb, each Circle requires up to half a day per week of facilitator time for the first two to three months of its existence, and then up to a quarter of a day a week for a further two to three months, after which it should have been developed to a stage where it is running independently. It should be noted that these figures represent the maximum time required, and can sometimes be reduced, but equally it must be recognised that time does need to be invested if the programme is to work.

The second main reason why Circles and Circle programmes occasionally founder is that those taking part in the programme do not make it easy enough for management, notably middle management, to relate to the programme and commit themselves to it. This is a trap to avoid if Circles are to succeed in the long run, and become a normal part of the way things are done in a company (see Chapter 10).

The third major cause of occasional failures lies in the fact that some companies have begun Quality Circles programmes without any real understanding of the nature of the concept. For them it has been either a management gimmick, good for a few months, or worth a try because it was new and appealing. Against such a background it is hardly surprising that their programmes have not stood the test of time. The concept of Quality Circles is much more subtle and delicate than at first meets the eye, and so it is to these nuances and to developing a broader understanding of the basis of the approach that we should now turn.

In 1960 a book called *The Human Side of Enterprise* was published. It was written by Douglas McGregor, and it propounded a philosophy which, although widely known, is very little understood. McGregor's Theory X and Theory Y describe two very different sets of assumptions that can be made about people at work which are both valuable in themselves and also relevant to an understanding of Quality Circles. McGregor conducted a programme of research in industry which led him to the conclusion that the assumptions made by managers about their job and their subordinates could be broadly categorised into one of two sets. By far the most common – indeed, he called it the traditional view of direction and control – was labelled Theory X. As a set of assumptions, Theory X fits comfortably with Taylorism; indeed, Scientific Management could be seen as the natural way a Theory X person would organise things. The assumptions which comprise Theory X are as follows:

1  The average human being has an inherent dislike of work and will avoid it if he can.

    This assumption is very firmly held by a very large number of people. Indeed, any questioning of it is often met with straightforward incredulity. It is pointed out that levels of absenteeism are high, and that proposed changes to improve the lot of staff are inevitably met with demands for more money. It is said that you only have to listen to the talk in the canteen, office or locker room to see that it is true. And the clincher is often, 'Would you carry on working if you won the football pools? Of course not!'

2  Because of this human characteristic of dislike of work, most people must be coerced, controlled, directed, or threatened with punishment to get them to put forth adequate effort towards the achievement of organisational objectives.

    This assumption is often 'verified' during periods of recession, when it is noted, often with glee, that the number of industrial disputes falls, and workpeople seem to 'toe the line' more readily.

3  The average human being prefers to be directed,

wishes to avoid responsibility, has relatively little ambition, wants security above all.

Again this assumption is very widely held. There are very many managers whose protestations of the worth of their people are in fact a thin veil over their paternalistic views. Paternalism, with its assumption that people in general are not capable of contributing usefully to decisions which affect their own destiny, is very much alive.

It is all too easy to be contemptuous of Theory X, dismissing it as a product of Neanderthal man, and nothing to do with modern-day business, but, as McGregor said, 'Theory X is not a straw man for purposes of demolition, but is in fact a theory which materially influences managerial strategy in a wide sector of ... industry today'.

A vital point about Theory X, however, is that it has not become the prevailing set of assumptions by accident. As McGregor says, 'Theory X provides an explanation of some human behaviour in industry. These assumptions would not have persisted if there were not a considerable body of evidence to support them'. He goes on, however, to explain that there is evidence of the possibility that another way of viewing man at work may have some utility. He says, 'Nevertheless, there are many readily observable phenomena in industry and elsewhere which are not consistent with this view of human nature.... Such a state of affairs is not uncommon. The history of science provides many examples of theoretical explanations which persist over long periods despite the fact that they are only partially adequate. Newton's laws of motion are a case in point. It was not until the development of the theory of relativity during the present century that important inconsistencies and inadequacies in Newtonian theory could be understood and corrected.'

In many cases the justification of Theory X is a self-fulfilling prophecy. People treated in such a way will respond likewise and provide the 'evidence' for the original set of assumptions. This was brought home vividly to one managing director, who went on a training course and at one particular stage of the proceedings was moved to say, 'The trouble with workers today is that 5 per cent of them work, 10 per cent of them think they work, and 85 per cent of them would rather die than work'. The trainer on the course suggested that he repeat what he had just said but add on the end the words 'in my company'. The managing director obliged and said, 'The trouble with workers today is that 5 per cent of them work, 10 per cent of them think they work, and 85 per cent of them would rather die than work in my company'. Having said this, the managing director in question gained a new insight into motivation and the impact of his own behaviour upon it.

McGregor's alternative set of assumptions, which he saw as being more productive in both business and human terms than the first, he named Theory Y. The six assumptions which comprise Theory Y are:

1   The expenditure of physical and mental effort in work is as natural as play or rest.

    McGregor explains: 'The average human being does not inherently dislike work. Depending upon controllable conditions, work may be a source of satisfaction (and will be voluntarily performed) or a source of punishment (and will be avoided if possible)'.
2   External control and the threat of punishment are not the only means of bringing about effort toward organisational objectives. Man will exercise self-direction and self-control in the service of objectives to which he is committed.
3   Commitment to objectives is a function of the rewards associated with their achievement.

    The rewards talked about here are not only material.

McGregor sees the needs for self-esteem and self-fulfilment as the most significant unsatisfied needs of the average working man.

4   The average human being learns, under proper conditions, not only to accept but to seek responsibility.

McGregor explains: 'Avoidance of responsibility, lack of ambition, and emphasis on security are generally consequences of experience, not inherent human characteristics.'

5   The capacity to exercise a relatively high degree of imagination, ingenuity and creativity in the solution of organisational problems is widely, not narrowly, distributed in the population.

6   Under the conditions of modern industrial life, the intellectual potentialities of the average human being are only partially utilised.

Before we move on to discuss the way Quality Circles fit into the theoretical framework of Theory Y, it is useful to recognise that Theory X can be very much more subtle than the raw assumptions might imply. In the days before legislation, trade-union power, and in some cases more enlightened management, it was much more possible for a 'hard' version of Theory X to be practised. 'Hard' in this respect does not, of course, mean difficult, for of all the managerial strategies, given the legal and organisational power with which to carry it out, this is the easiest and least demanding style of management possible. It expects nothing of the subordinate, and therefore puts no demands on the manager in  terms of the process of managing. The reason why such managers invariably overwork is because they do everything themselves, since 'you can't trust anyone to do anything around here'.

When social and legal circumstances changed, Theory X did not die; chameleonlike, it changed its shade. With the emergence of 'human relations' as an issue on a wide scale it became fashionable to think in terms of human motivation in rather less crude terms than 'the stick and the carrot', to talk about the worth of the individual, to try and tap his potential by finding devices to make him more interested in his work, and to enthuse him by various communication devices. If we look beneath the surface of these activities, it quickly becomes apparent that on many occasions they were actually a mechanism for getting people to work, based on the assumption that people will avoid it if they can; that they represented a manipulative device to get people to put forth effort in the service of organisational objectives, while management owned the activities, made up the rules, and decided who would be allowed to 'play the game'. In other words, Theory X was being practised under a different guise. This 'soft' Theory X is very dangerous, since it is often claimed by practitioners to be Theory Y.

Theory Y above all else has high expectations of people's ability and willingness to solve their own problems when given appropriate conditions. Of all the managerial styles, it is by far the most demanding and stretching for the manager, not only in creating the environment where it can flourish, but in managing the outcomes of such a dynamic process with a wide range of people thinking, questioning and improving the way things are done. The many managers and companies who are actively seeking to create and work within the framework of Theory Y will testify to the demands made upon them, but few, if any, will consider changing, for, in the longer term, it works not only in terms of tangible results but also in terms of the many other benefits which accrue to staff and managers alike.

It is easy to see that Quality Circles can be fitted into either a Theory X or Theory Y model. This is a very serious issue for consideration by any company thinking of introducing the idea. A Theory X company will perceive Quality Circles as devices for making people think they are participating in the generation of a range of improvements at the workplace. They will tend to see it as something that will last for a while and then quietly fizzle out.

It will not be possible to dissuade some of these companies from introducing Circles, and there is a danger
that their experience will influence companies which
introduce the concept on a very different basis. It is
salutary to consider the perceptions of staff at the start of
Quality Circles programmes and to note that their biggest
worry is that the Theory X situation will occur. They have
a very clear perception as to what this will mean for their
own motivation, and for any future attempts the company
might make to 'trick' them into believing they were being
treated as adults.

On the other hand, it is hoped that the majority of companies that introduce Quality Circles will do so from a
genuine Theory Y perspective. That Quality Circles do fit
within a Theory Y perspective is undeniable: it is only
necessary to consider the philosophy and ground rules of
the Quality Circle approach and compare them with the
six principles of Theory Y to see that the two go hand in
glove. McGregor's book predates the first Quality Circle
by two years, and, whether or not this is significant, there
is little doubt that McGregor would support the concept
as being wholly in line with the philosophies he
espoused.

Looking at Quality Circles programmes that have
already been introduced, one is indeed forcibly struck by
the link. There are always enough people who volunteer
to join in, and they need no payment, threat or promise
other than being treated like intelligent human beings.
The groups which are formed are happy to take the
responsibility of solving their own problems, and they do
so, often in remarkably creative and ingenious ways.
There are few people who have in any way taken part in,
or simply seen, the development of a Quality Circle
programme who would not readily agree that, 'Under the
conditions of modern industrial life, the intellectual
potentialities of the average human being are only
partially utilised'.

In this chapter we have traced the history and the theoretical basis of Quality Circles. Strangely, the origins are separate from the best available explanation of their basis. There is talk among some people of Quality Circles being culturally based, and only possible in the East. This, given the discussion of McGregor's theory, is patently not true. Indeed, if there were to have been a cultural problem, it should have been the other way round , since Quality Circles are firmly based on modern Western behavioural knowledge.

## Further reading

Deming, W. E., *Sample Designs in Business Research,* John Wiley & Sons, New York, 1960.

Juran, J. M., *Quality Control Handbook,* McGraw-Hill, 1974.

Taylor, F. W., *Scientific Management,* Greenwood Press, London, 1972.

# Chapter 3

# THE CORE
# PRINCIPLES

Any technique or philosophy contains assumptions and underlying principles which it is necessary to understand if the concept is to be applied in a controlled way. Quality Circles, as has been said before, are deceptively simple, and there are in fact a number of quite complex principles which underpin the technique. Without a knowledge and understanding of these it will not be possible to implement Quality Circles in anything but a simplistic way, and clearly this unpreparedness will be likely to prevent the approach fulfilling its real potential. This chapter explains the key principles of Quality Circles.

## Voluntariness

The principle of voluntariness is very much at the centre of Quality Circles. It is the most important rule, yet it is very often misunderstood, by management and staff alike, because it is such an unusual feature in our working lives, in which very little can be said to be truly voluntary. There are a number of practical guidelines that are vital to the operation of the principle, and the first is that it operates at all levels. Clearly the managing director of any company decides whether or not he wishes to try the concept, and, in consequence, is a volunteer; and similarly staff who come forward to join the groups do so on an entirely voluntary basis. In addition, the Circle leader, who is the first-line supervisor in the section concerned, must be a volunteer also. He or she must volunteer before the staff are asked, since the setting up of a group in any area is contingent upon the supervisor wanting to. Furthermore, the wishes of any middle managers who do not want Circles in their departments must be respected, though they are usually willing for at least a limited experiment to be carried out, to evaluate the concept, even if some of them are sceptical in the beginning.

Because everyone who participates has to volunteer, it is necessary to structure the introduction of the concept into a company, basically by cascading it down the organisation. Such an introduction avoids raising the expectations of staff who may work in areas where supervision or management is opposed to the idea. A corollary of voluntariness is that there will be people who do not wish to join in, and this is a vital strength. If anyone were to claim that he had a highly successful Circle programme which included everyone in his company, it would be highly unlikely that he had a Circle programme at all, since the likelihood of all the staff of a company volunteering is very low. A second corollary of voluntariness is respect for different views. For a company to say to its employees that it respects their opinions as to whether or not they wish to join in will come as a surprise to many of them, but the confidence that comes out of the knowledge that one's views will be respected is a key outcome of many Quality Circles programmes.

The second important practicality regarding voluntariness is that it operates on a week-to-week basis, so everyone, at least technically, volunteers anew for each meeting. This freedom has the effect of ensuring that commitment is kept at a high level if the Circles are to be continued. In fact, people tend to come along to the next meeting automatically, but the basis on which the Circles are set up should be made clear at the outset.

The principle of voluntariness is vital at all levels of the organisation if Quality Circles are to succeed. To understand why this is the case, it is necessary to understand attitudes and how they are influenced.

An attitude can be defined as a predisposition to evaluate something or someone in a favourable or unfavourable light. There are two clear parts of an attitude: one is the so-called cognitive component, which is what someone thinks, knows or has experienced about a subject or person; and the second is the affective component, which encompasses all our feelings about the person or issue. A third dimension which needs to be taken into account, the conative component, includes how someone is predisposed to act as a result of his thoughts and feelings. Some researchers have concluded that this behavioural dimension is a true part of our attitude, whereas others prefer to keep it separate. Suffice it to say that, all other things being equal, there is likely to be a high correlation between our attitudes and our behaviour.

Once we understand what our attitudes consist of, it is useful to move on a stage further to the prediction that people in general prefer to be consistent in what they think, feel and do; that is, they like to keep the different parts of their attitude, and their behaviour, in some kind of balance. Inconsistency leads to feelings of discomfort, which most people will act to reduce. Examples are all around us. During a recent petrol shortage a taxi driver said he would never go to a certain garage again because the owner was profiteering. A month later, having been 'forced' to buy petrol from the garage because it was unavailable elsewhere, the same taxi driver explained that it was really quite a good garage, for, although it was a bit expensive, at least you could always get petrol there! He had rationalised his thoughts and feelings to bring them into line with his behaviour.

Another example concerns a couple who were opposed to private education before they moved to an area where the state system was very poor. Their views then began to change, as they explained that one should not let the children suffer for a principle; it was a terrible shame there was a need for private education but the inadequacies of the state system were such that in certain areas there was no alternative.

A third example concerns a businessman who, after months of detailed preparation, failed to secure a long-term contract with a major buyer. His reaction was to explain that it was a blessing in disguise, since to have won the order would probably have had a serious effect on his cash flow, which might have ended in his going bankrupt. Here he was adapting his thoughts and feelings in line with the reality of having failed to achieve the desired outcome.

This juggling with our thoughts, feelings and behaviour is an integral part of life. Understanding the process is also a vital part of understanding organisational behaviour, especially when taken in conjunction with the theory of cognitive dissonance introduced by Leon Festinger in 1957. Festinger stated that if a person is induced to say or do something contrary to his private attitude, he will tend to modify his thoughts and feelings to bring them into line with his new behaviour. He adds an important rider, however, which is that the greater the pressure used to bring about the change of attitude (thoughts and feelings), beyond the minimum amount needed to produce it, the less the attitude will change. Although in many ways simple, this theory has great power, and can help us to understand many of the apparently strange reactions of people both at work and outside.

For example, interpreting the demise of many management-by-objectives programmes by means of this theory, we can point to the usual method of introduction as being a serious mistake. Most management-by-objectives programmes were imposed, and the whole of the management structure had to adapt its behaviour to use the prescribed forms and go through the process demanded by the system. People had no choice. In Festinger's terms people had been induced to behave contrary to their private attitude, since if it had been their attitude to support MBO initially, they would probably have been using the system already. In such circumstances, as Festinger explains, a low level of dissonance is aroused, since people can simply shrug their shoulders and say, 'It's nothing to do with me, I'm just doing as I'm told'. Given this kind of situation, there is little attitude change; people will simply take the first opportunity to change their behaviour back to fit in with their original attitudes. This is a very compelling explanation of why so many changes fail to stand the test of time, and certainly the history of management by objectives can be convincingly explained in this way.

It is easy, therefore, to understand the importance of the voluntary principle in Quality Circles. If something is voluntary, clearly there is no pressure put on anyone to join in, the commitment of anyone who chooses to join will be high, and their attitude is likely to fall in line behind the new behaviour. In this case, in terms of Festinger's theory, a high level of dissonance is aroused, leading to a high likelihood of attitude change, whether it be among staff or any level of management. The fact that no pressure is brought to bear ensures at least that there is none of the kind of rejection that has been so much a feature of other programmes.

Voluntariness is essential to the concept under discussion. Without it, whatever we have, we do not have Quality Circles. The voluntary principle makes both theoretical and common sense. With it, we have the commitment of participants who choose to use their skills to solve their problems rather than avoid them either by blaming someone else or by explaining that it is not their job to solve them. Quality Circles are not a trick. In the long run they can only work if they are based on respect between people who are paid to do different jobs and yet who choose to work towards an environment in which it is possible for everyone to win, and ultimately to share the benefits of jointly earned success.

## Whose problems?

In many companies the problem-solving, or rather problem-avoiding, ethic is to point fingers at other people or departments and blame it all on them. Where this happens, the net result is that fewer problems are tackled, morale suffers and the performance of the company is adversely affected. The habit of blaming it all on other people is deeply engrained in many of us and is not easy to eradicate. It is a syndrome which is widely experienced across companies, and one we could all do without. Quality Circles help to reduce the amount of unproductive finger-pointing because their brief is to solve their own problems, not the next department's, the company's or the world's. The phrase which will be heard time and time again in respect of Circles is that they 'put their own house in order', and this makes a tremendous difference both to attitudes and to the number of problems tackled. Circle members are no different from anyone else. Generally they begin by wanting everyone else to change because 'it's all their fault', but, thanks to the training and the back-up support they receive, they begin to see problems in terms of what they can do about them, they stop pointing fingers and so they are able to get things done.

An important corollary of this aspect of Circles is that, in solving their own problems – the things that go wrong at the workplace – they usually free management to focus on other matters. In the past, management will have felt it necessary to try to solve the problems the Circles are now solving, not because managers wanted to, or because it was their job, but because the problems needed solving and no one else seemed to be willing or able to do it.

Often managers have become so accustomed to filling this role that they initially see Quality Circles as impinging on them, and will make such remarks as, 'They won't achieve anything that isn't done at present'. The point here, of course, is that if these groups can solve their own problems at their own level, they will be giving the manager time to concentrate on broader issues which he might have had insufficient time to tackle fully in the past (see Chapter 10). Managers should be encouraged to think of the core principle of Quality Circles, 'putting their own house in order', as being, among other things, a mechanism for enabling them to spend more time on tackling issues at their level, rather than having to spend it solving other people's problems.

A question often asked in this context is what happens when the group runs out of problems, to which a threefold answer may be given. Firstly, Circles usually surprise themselves when it comes to recognising how many problems they have the potential to influence, and solve, at least in part. The brainstorm lists that Circles generate frequently contain eighty to a hundred problems which the group sees itself as capable of influencing. Even given that a proportion of these are likely to be outside the control of the Circle, and others are either trivial or unsolvable for one reason or another, there is invariably plenty to do.

Secondly, once the groups have developed their skills at problem-solving, and, importantly, when they are no longer predisposed to point fingers at other people and departments, they are ready to start phase two of Circle working, which includes tackling interface problems with other Circles, sections or groups. This stage must not be rushed, for if the finger-pointing ethic is still there, disaster will inevitably result. It would be surprising if many groups were ready for this step within, say, two years, and in any case, most groups have enough problems and opportunities to work on to keep them productively occupied for at least this amount of time. This development is something of a quantum leap in terms of the types of issue that can be tackled, and there is often a temptation to rush it. Don't!

Thirdly, although Circles begin by tackling immediate and pressing problems in the workplace, they should be encouraged to widen their horizons and look also for opportunities to make improvements in their section, even if current performance is satisfactory. There are always opportunities to improve the quality of output and to reduce waste. Circles are in an ideal position to work on such improvements, and projects such as these need never come to an end.

In summary, then, a vital principle of the Quality Circle approach is that it focuses attention on the things we can do something about. It is easy to make a long list of problems for other people to solve. For Circles the list of problems is only the first stage of the problem-solving process; they must then go on to identify what they can influence, select their problem, analyse and solve it in an organised, data-based way, and sell their solution to management, which has the task of making a decision. If the solution is accepted, the group implements it and monitors results. The approach is effective because things get done, and more time is made available because more people are helping to tackle the problems they can really solve – their own.

## Ownership

The question of ownership in relation to Quality Circles is more complex than might be thought. At one level it is simple and obvious – the Circles themselves must own the process. But it is not as straightforward as this either in theory or in practice.

As has already been stressed, Quality Circles are entirely voluntary in terms of membership. This factor undoubtedly results in a high level of commitment among those who do volunteer, and high commitment leads to a feeling of ownership – to be encouraged, as Circles will not endure unless they are owned by the members. There is a danger, however, that this ownership may be perceived as a threat by line management above the Circle: after all, the manager, if he is to be effective, must feel a sense of ownership for his whole department. At first glance this duality of ownership seems to be somewhat of a paradox, and indeed it is a situation that has caused problems with some Circle programmes, especially where all the attention has been concentrated on developing the Circle members' ownership. Quite understandably in such circumstances, management can begin to feel either threatened or resentful. Although this has happened on occasions, it is not inevitable; indeed, it is possible not only to avoid the problem, but also to make a positive strength out of a duality of ownership, since this publicly recognises the commitment needed to make the approach work, and disposes of one of the most serious worries that arise at the outset of most introductory programmes. Ownership, therefore, must be vested in the Circle itself as far as the workings of the groups are concerned. It is for members to decide the problem they wish to tackle, how they tackle it and what solution they come up with. There are few restrictions to bind them – ultimately the only one is that they have to reap what they sow. If they insist on producing opinion-based solutions to problems outside their control, two things are likely to happen: one, they will not be listened to, and, two, the group will fold up. That is the real world. Equally, and, experience shows, infinitely more likely, if they produce data-based arguments to solve their own problems, they will build up an enhanced respect for their abilities and get things done. Again, that is the real world.

Line management's ownership must lie in support for the concept of Quality Circles as an integral part of a way of managing. This support need not be fully present at the beginning, since a degree of scepticism will be understandable in many environments. What is important, however, is that the line managers are flexible enough to allow the approach to be integrated as part of the normal style of managing if it succeeds. Experience shows that all but the weakest and least confident of managers have this flexibility, if they can turn away from the debilitating aspects of history and frustration which are so prominent in the minds of many people at all levels of organisations. The simplest definition of management, which is learned by 9.15 am on the first day of any course on the subject, is that it is a process of 'getting things done through people'. Quality Circles help make this process easier, because staff want to take the opportunity to get things done. That they will take the opportunity and work at it in the long term says a lot about their managers. People do not choose to do things they regard as a waste of time.

A different aspect of ownership, which it is important to consider, is concealment of ownership. It is vital for the success of a programme that the company is not using Quality Circles as a manipulative device to get more out of the workforce. Further than this, it is essential that no one in the company perceives that this is the case. If the ownership is perceived to be with management – if, in other words, it is thought that management is 'pulling the strings' – the programme is unlikely to make much headway, and does not deserve to. Equally, if management is perceived to take all the credit, given early success, the same outcome can be predicted. Quality Circles are intended to enable staff to use the abilities they possess. The effect of so-called Scientific Management has been to reduce the opportunity for staff to use all their skills, and, in general, management has had little opportunity to change this. Quality Circles, however, offer a mechanism for helping everyone to win, and any one party attempting to take all the kudos does so at its own risk and that of the whole programme.

## The adult–adult contract

It may seem obvious to say so, but Quality Circle members are adults and should be treated as such. This is a very serious point, since there is sometimes a temptation for people dealing with staff, both in Circles and outside, to treat them almost as children. There is little more infuriating to most people than this attitude, and it is to be avoided at all costs. There are three likely 'danger points' for lapsing into the paternalistic role.

The first of these is that management might be tempted to give praise where none is due – for example, at management presentations. There is no point in saying that something is good if quite clearly it is not. Praise should be given where it is deserved, otherwise the value of the whole process of reinforcing positive contributions becomes meaningless. Another danger point comes in the preparation and review meetings held between the leader and facilitator. Here the danger is twofold: firstly, that the facilitator may assume a parental relationship towards the leader; and, secondly, that the two of them combine and adopt this attitude towards the group. A third danger is that the Circle may find itself playing a 'child' role and thereby invite a paternalistic response, especially in the early days. When this happens, the group needs careful handling to bring it out of its dependency. It would be very unwise in such circumstances, for example, simply to say 'Grow up!', and expect that to do the trick. Care and honesty are also required in diagnosing unhelpful 'parent–child' relationships between leader and facilitator. No one enjoys being confronted by such an accusation, and tactless handling may well result in further 'parent–child' behaviour.

Careful consideration of the need to treat people as adults should be built into the training given to leaders and facilitators, and this is probably the best preventive measure available. Awareness of the dangers is at least half the battle, and, given this knowledge, most people will avoid most of the danger for most of the time.

## Data-based problem-solving

An important principle of Quality Circles, which is at the root of much of the effective work of the groups in their problem-solving activities, is the notion that solutions should be based on facts rather than opinions. Such a principle often demands a radical change in the way problems are handled, since in many companies opinion-based argument is the norm, the resultant conflict and frustration being very difficult to resolve. People will usually claim that their knowledge and experience are a sufficient basis for action. 'I've been here for twenty years and I'm telling you, the only answer is to buy a new machine!' Comments like this are heard in virtually every company, and are examples of exactly the kinds of contribution that lead to frustration. It would be unthinkable for any competent manager to act merely on such 'evidence', yet there is often little understanding of the reasons for rejecting such proposals.

Quality Circles help to improve this situation through the training given to leaders and members alike. The recommended problem-solving structure places a heavy emphasis on data collection, for which training is given, as well as on the principle of the cost/benefit ratio and payback periods. Interestingly enough, there is rarely any rejection of this new way of approaching problem-solving; indeed, most groups get an additional kick out of being able to quantify the benefits of their work, and become firmly committed to the data-based approach. This commitment obviously helps to make it easier to get things done. The manager mentioned above will find it easy to make the decision about the new machine if presented with the facts of the situation. In addition, through this mechanism, management and staff suddenly start talking the same language. Quality Circles play an important part in the improvement of communication by providing a common language to be used in approaching and solving problems.

## Realistic time perspective

As a result of the way most companies are structured there could be said to be a direct correlation between the hierarchical level of the job and the time perspective required to fulfil it. Whereas the managing director's concerns may span several years, the equivalent time frame for the operator on a short-cycle machine could be a matter of seconds. This difference can spill over into the expectation held by people in general concerning the length of time required to get things to happen, and very often it is the real cause of problems of communication between different levels of the business.

Developing realistic time perspectives is an important part of living in the real world, and Quality Circles can help to facilitate this process. At the beginning of Circle programmes group members are generally impatient to get things done and worried that 'nothing will happen'. A part of this concern is to do with the commonly held notion that things can and should change overnight. People point to other interventions where expectations of progress were raised and then dashed and ask whether Quality Circles will suffer the same fate. The collapse of many such programmes, however, owed more to the hope of too much too soon than anything else, and Quality Circles avoid this trap by building a recognition from the start of the need to live in the real world. Everything takes time, and the bigger the problem being tackled the more time it is likely to take, not only its implementation but also the procedures needed to ensure that a correct decision is made to start with.

The development of realistic and matching time perspectives at all levels of the business is another valuable aid in ensuring effective communications, as well as being vital for the success of Quality Circles. It is something that itself takes time to emerge.

## Win/win

At the very heart of the Quality Circles philosophy is the belief that it is possible and desirable to build a situation in which healthy competition thrives yet where the efforts of employees are based on collaboration and on everyone winning. Such an aim is in stark contrast to the situation prevailing in so many companies, where unproductive 'us and them' conflict exists between sections, departments and different levels in the business, usually management and staff. Unproductive competition, so-called win/lose, is all around. Indeed, it is probably the rule rather than the exception in many businesses, and to understand the full potential of the Quality Circles approach it is necessary to have a clear appreciation of this whole attitude.

The first thing that needs to be quite clear is the distinction between healthy and unhealthy competition. So much of our lives is concerned with competition of one sort or another that there is often a tendency to view it as intrinsically good. It seems healthy and sensible that sports teams go out to try to defeat each other, since there would be little point in playing if the only acceptable results were a draw or tie! The legal system demands verdicts of innocence or guilt, winning and losing. People who apply for jobs in competition with each other either succeed or fail. Companies persuade the public to buy their own products as opposed to those of their competitors. There are numerous situations in which it is easy to conclude that competition is healthy and a good thing, but this is not always the case. The 'competition' between departments based on each side attempting to gain 'brownie points' at the expense of the other can only lessen the effectiveness of the company, and so it is between any section, group or individuals.

The debilitating aspects of win/lose are impossible to quantify, but, undoubtedly, they are the biggest single cause of the sub-optimal performance of organisations. In working towards a win/win situation the organisation opens up the possibilities of achieving synergy, a result which exceeds the sum of the inputs, for example, $1 + 1 = 3$. We all know of examples of teams which, although they contain no 'stars', combine so well that they 'win the league'. These are often practical examples of synergy being achieved. Viewing organisations in these terms is truly exciting, if rather daunting. Achieving an output which is better than the sum total of the abilities of the people and constituents of the company would put most of our businesses in a different ball game, let alone a different league! So the potential of achieving win/win is immense. The alternative is a situation where compromise and negativism rule the day and where everything reduces to the level of the lowest common denominator. The real problem with unhealthy win/lose is that it very rarely leads to anyone winning anything but the most fleeting of triumphs. The loser can so easily make the price of winning very high, and can transform a win/lose situation into one in which everyone loses. Such is the outcome of every 'us and them' situation that exists, whether it be between management and unions, production and sales, you and me. The question is whether it is realistic to think that this 'norm' can be changed, for there is no point in investing the time and effort required over the necessary period of time if there is no expectation of success.

In fact, there are enough examples of companies that have developed themselves into genuinely collaborative units to give the encouragement to try. Not that the task is straightforward or that results can be achieved overnight; in large companies it will take years. It is worthwhile, however, because of the huge difference the change makes, progressively, to the performance of the company in all aspects of its endeavour. Clearly it would be unrealistic to expect every single person in a company of any size to play a full part in the collaborative effort. But it is entirely reasonable to expect that, given the right conditions, developed and maintained over a sufficient period of time, most people will be prepared to work collaboratively to achieve the organisation's goals. 'Right conditions' includes developing the employees' ownership of the business and building in suitable mechanisms to facilitate their influencing the parts of the business where they can have some real effect. In such a situation Quality Circles can be powerful and effective. The approach is not an end in itself, but rather a means of achieving other goals, mainly to change the culture of a win/lose organisation into one of collaboration based on win/win.

The whole philosophy centres on participation and collaboration, which does not mean everyone having a say in every decision that is made. That would lead to chaos. The participation and collaboration necessary are of an infinitely more practical kind, and, surprisingly enough, are more acceptable to everyone. They are based on the premise that people can contribute optimally not only, or even necessarily, by working harder, but by working more cleverly. This implies using our skills, experience and abilities to solve the problems of our own workplace, ensuring that 'our end' of the interface with other departments is sound and being able to feel confident that people in other sections or departments, and at other levels of the organisation, are doing the same.

Quality Circles are an immensely powerful way of assisting this whole process. They develop the philosophy of win/win among staff who choose to take part, and enable people to put it into practice. They are an essential ingredient of the philosophy being propounded, since an enabling mechanism is needed for staff participation, and Quality Circles are by far the best one available.

## Further reading

Festinger, Leon, *A Theory of Cognitive Dissonance*, Harper and Row, New York, 1957.

# Chapter 4

# WHY BOTHER?

There is no doubt that many people find the idea of Quality Circles both interesting and appealing in an intuitive sense, and were it to cost nothing to introduce, there would possibly be less need to explore the potential benefits in depth. Quality Circles, however, do not come free. To implement an effective programme will almost certainly involve spending money on training material and perhaps specialist outside resources; but even if these costs are avoided, there is still the investment of time needed for Circles to meet. Since both time and money are scarce resources, any competent management must ensure that the investment of either pays the requisite dividend. Quality Circles should certainly not be introduced because they 'sounded like a good idea at the time'. Careful thought needs to be given to the likely outcomes.

Quality Circles are an interesting approach in many ways, not least that they can work at a number of levels and be aimed at a number of apparently quite different objectives. Some of the potential benefits are relatively small, whereas others can affect the whole organisation; some are tangible, others are more diffuse and qualitative. All deserve consideration.

## Theory Y
This term is intended here to be a 'catch all' to indicate a way of running a business, a way of managing, that assumes most people to have a considerable range and depth of abilities which they will be prepared to use to

51

help achieve organisational objectives, as long as the 'rules of the game' are conducive. Quality Circles cannot achieve this entirely on their own, but have a vital part to play in helping to make the theory really work in practice, especially at the level of junior management and staff.

Since its inception over twenty years ago, the principles underlying Theory Y have been debated *ad nauseam*. There have been many attempts to change organisations in order to tap the potential highlighted by McGregor, and it would be fair to say that few of the attempts have fully achieved the goal, although many would claim, justifiably, to have made inroads in what is an enormously difficult task. Job enrichment and quality of working life schemes, work organisation and organisation development programmes, to name but a few, have all been a part of this quest for improvement, and now Quality Circles is playing its part in many companies. Organisations that have espoused the concept in its entirety have found, and are still finding, that it is an approach with a long, even indefinite, life span, in contrast to many of the other approaches, which have failed to stand the test of time. The main reason for the success of Quality Circles is that they give non-managerial staff, with their first-line supervisor, the opportunity of contributing to the creation of a more successful organisation and a more satisfactory working life.

## Communication

Whether or not the world would beat a path to the door of the person who invented a better mousetrap is, to say the least, a moot point. It is rather more certain that the managing directors of the world would rush to anyone who invented a perfect means of communication. Let us hasten to add that Quality Circles do not aspire to the role: perfection is a big word. The approach does, however, have something to offer.

In any diagnosis of problems and areas of possible

improvement in companies of any size the word communications is almost bound to come up; indeed, in many cases it will be deemed to be the major problem. Of course, the word itself covers a multitude of sins and requires careful definition if it is to mean anything useful. Nonetheless, it is a word that is of the utmost importance in organisations today.

Over the past couple of decades an increasing amount of attention has been paid to the subject of communicating within organisations, along with increased attention to the human resource. Whatever the morality of present or past styles, in practical terms communication has become more important, as have improvements in educational standards, changing and more liberal values, and also social legislation.

The response to this pressure to communicate has been interesting if only because it has taken such different forms in different organisations. At one end of the spectrum of communication devices is the annual report for the staff – the glossy brochure full of pie charts and explanations of how good or bad a year it has been and the reasons why – and undoubtedly this has a role to play in ensuring that company results are at least made available to staff in a digestible form. A very different device is briefing groups. Here groups of staff, usually within their own work groups, are brought together regularly to be told of any important 'news' that has happened since the last briefing, and to have the opportunity to ask questions. There are also, of course, countless other communication mechanisms of more or less formality, and they all play their part in trying to transfer relevant information to staff.

One of the 'missing links' in many businesses to date, however, has been a system which enables a genuine two-way flow of information to take place, an increasingly important consideration as the organisation increases in size and the problems of communications become correspondingly greater. The two devices out-lined above, commendable though they are, do not really fill the role, and much time, effort and resources have been invested by many organisations in devising and implementing mechanisms of communications in an attempt to improve the flow of information both to and from staff. Now Quality Circles can fill this gap. Because the approach uses natural work groups, it provides the opportunity for communication to take place in its 'natural' setting, and this is a key to success. Experience indicates that after a while Circles often broaden the scope of their meetings and use them to feed back infor-mation to the supervisor on various important issues con-cerning his approach and style outside the Circle, and also to receive feedback of a similar nature from the leader himself. Thus, as well as retaining their problem-solving role, the groups take on additional tasks related to communicating their view upwards and receiving comment themselves. Information flow such as this can only occur within a natural work group, and is, therefore, an additional benefit that comes out of the particular composition of the groups. Genuine two-way com-munication will only take place in an atmosphere of mutual trust and respect, and this has to be earned by all parties. There are many reasons why there is so little straight talking between levels of organisations, including the lack of the kind of trust and respect which has just been referred to. It is a tribute, therefore, to the members of the groups and the approach that they develop these attributes and are able to put them to good use.

It must be recognised, however, in considering the role of Quality Circles as communication devices, that it is complementary to other mechanisms being employed; it does not replace them, since it tackles a different part of the need. Apart from anything else, the voluntary approach will not ensure a full coverage of staff.

## Management and supervisor development

One of the biggest and most compelling benefits to come out of Quality Circles is the role it can play in the development of the managers and supervisors who choose to join in; indeed, there have been companies for which this has been the prime motivation for introducing the approach. Taking the supervisor first, there is little doubt that in many industries his role has been seriously weakened over the past two to three decades. One of the reasons has been the increase in social legislation, which has removed much of the obvious coercive power from the position. For example, it is usually no longer within the scope of the supervisor to 'hire and fire'. Another reason which has contributed in some organisations has been the rise of the influence of union officials, sometimes to the extent that they fulfil many of the tasks previously associated with the supervisor role.

Against this background Quality Circles do much to help the supervisor regain his legitimate role as the leader of the work group. They do not give him back the power to coerce his staff, but something much more valuable, which is to develop power bases far more appropriate to the managerial task today – specifically, the roles of knowledgeable leader in the sense of his developing and running an effective problem-solving group, and that of legitimate leader of the work group itself. Thus, less reliance needs to be placed on the structural authority vested in him by the company.

It is important to understand the dynamics of this process so that it can be managed effectively. It centres around developing the supervisor in the active role of Circle leader. The process of conducting training sessions and managing the problem-solving activities of the group invariably leads to increases in confidence. Such confidence is apparent to the Circle members who, therefore, begin to respect the leader within the group, a respect reinforced as the group's achievements accumulate. Since it would be psychologically uncomfortable to respect the supervisor for one hour a week and despise him for the rest of the time, the tendency is to begin to view his general performance with respect. The supervisor's confidence in his role is consequently strengthened, which helps lead to the development of improved competence. The level of competence is also developed by the technical knowledge gained from the Quality Circle training he will have received, specifically in the areas of problem-solving and dealing with his staff. The managers who volunteer to become facilitators also tend to find that their exposure to Circles in the role of 'helper' develops their skills, particularly those of man-management, and that these increased skills can be applied in their day-to-day performance in their line role.

## Quality of output

Quality Circles are about improving the quality of work in its widest sense. They are not limited to trying to make improvements in product quality, and indeed many of the problems chosen by the groups do relate to other aspects. But the quality of the output in the section whose Circles are operating almost invariably improves, whether or not the group tackles the issues specifically. This phenomenon is related to the increased interest in the job and pride of workmanship which are stimulated by the Quality Circle approach, and which have an effect during the whole of the week, not just during the hour of the Circle meeting.

## Cost-effectiveness

Quality Circles represent an investment. They cost time and money and thus need to be judged alongside other possible ways of allocating the necessary resources. Many of the benefits of the approach are not readily quantifiable, as will have been already appreciated. Although some companies claim not to be concerned about the tangible payback of introducing the concept, preferring to focus attention on such other benefits as supervisor development, participation and improved communications, most organisations will feature the economic benefits somewhere in their list of priorities.

In fact, Quality Circles, among their other virtues, make undeniable sense economically. Experience from all over the world indicates that the costs involved in running Circles will be repaid between five and eight times on an annual basis, and some companies claim payback ratios of up to 15:1 per annum.

## Participation

The opportunity the approach gives to all members of the company to participate is a further major benefit of Quality Circles. There have been many attempts at staff participation, and few of them have had real success. So-called 'worker directors' might be all right for the one or two people appointed, but can hardly be said to affect staff on a wide scale, and the same can be said of the various sorts of consultative committees which exist in many companies.

The great advantage of Quality Circles as a mechanism is that, ultimately, it gives everyone the chance to join in, but puts no pressure on them to do so. Furthermore, the sort of participation offered is highly practical and useful. It does not take the member of staff away from his area of expertise; it invites him, rather, to use his accumulated knowledge and experience to make things better in his section. It is this kind of participation which attracts the support of management, unions and staff alike, since it avoids the dangers of the 'ivory tower', gives work an added dimension of interest, and, moreover, gets things done. Arguably Quality Circles are the only approach offering the opportunity of meaningful staff participation on a wide scale, and the benefits are, of course, likely to be huge for all concerned.

The Quality Circle approach generates benefits for everyone who chooses to take part in it, and for the company as well. It is not a panacea for all the problems of the organisation, but it can play an important role in helping the business to move forward. Achieving the full potential of Quality Circles is likely to take a long time, but there are many benefits to be gained on the way to this long-term goal. Quality Circles are worth bothering about because they work. They work for the benefit of the company and all its staff.

# Part II
# INTRODUCING A QUALITY CIRCLES PROGRAMME

# Chapter 5

# THE BASIC REQUIREMENTS

As one would expect, there are a number of basic requirements for the successful introduction of a Quality Circles programme. It is all too easy to treat the concept as simple and self-evident, and what generally happens if this is done is that, after an initial flourish, the programme begins to languish and fail, amid accusations from all parties of inadequacies and neglect. Everyone ends in a worse position than before. Two steps forward and three steps back is no way to run anything!

## Commitment from the top
The need for commitment from senior management is a much quoted requirement; indeed, in one sense, it is a prerequisite of any in-company initiative. In many senses, and at the outset, it is the commitment which is easiest given by senior management and least believed by everyone else in the company. This is not meant as an indictment of senior management, rather as a comment on the complexity of life in general. Commitment has two aspects: firstly, and self-evidently, if there is insufficient management willingness at the start, a Quality Circles programme will never start, or perhaps even be considered; and, secondly, if the perceptions that others have of that management commitment are not favourable, then to all intents and purposes it may as well never have been given. The problem from the senior managers' perspective is not so much that of giving initial commitment

as of sticking to it publicly. A senior manager faces many and varied pressures on his time, and these pressures change with the many different issues that have to be dealt with. There is no doubt that many different kinds of initiative have foundered on the staff's perception that other priorities have weakened management's commitment to a particular programme. It is this second problem, that of the perception held by others of the commitment of their senior managers, which is likely to wreck a programme, and is, therefore, worth exploring further. Quality Circle members very often during their first few meetings have a high degree of anxiety about the whole programme, since they have 'put their necks on the block' by volunteering. They are likely to have colleagues who will be unconvinced about the validity of the concept, so it is understandable that they might feel they have gone out on a limb, to a certain extent at least. The most usual way of expressing this difficulty is to explain that protestations of commitment have been heard before and have fizzled out after a few months. An often heard comment is, 'It's all very well now, while the whole thing is in the limelight, to talk about commitment, but what will happen in six months' time when something else is happening?' The confidence of participants in the sustained commitment of top management is a key factor.

This observation is substantiated by the findings of much motivational research. For example, Victor Vroom, who has done much work on the subject of motivation, found that the effort put into anything was a function of the desire for the outcome multiplied by the expectation that exerting effort would lead to the desired outcome. This finding can assist our understanding not only of Quality Circles but of human motivation and behaviour in general. In terms of Quality Circles it implies that members of staff can have a very high desire to contribute in working towards the Company's future, but if they have no expectation that their efforts will lead to the desired outcome, they will not bother. An obvious example of this most common of characteristics concerns the football pools. Many people have a very high desire to win the pools and yet do not fill in a coupon regularly, not because their desire is any the less in the weeks when they forget to fill out the form, but because their expectation of actually winning is very low. Thus, a high desire to win multiplied by an almost nil expectation of success leads to low effort: result, forgetfulness, occasionally with disastrous results, as the popular newspapers will be keen to report.

The results of making assumptions about the apparent lack of effort put in by some people at work can be equally disastrous. So often one hears condemnation of staff who appear to be apathetic and negative. In such circumstances it is worth considering that those concerned could have a very high desire to be positive and committed but a very low expectation that effort on their part would lead to any useful result. Where this is so, the responsibility for creating an environment wherein staff have a high expectation of success lies usually with senior management.

The requirement in terms of top management support, therefore, is that other participants in the programme perceive that the support is there and will remain there. Senior people who are not only committed but can generate a belief in this commitment will provide a foundation of confidence that will stand the Circles programme in good stead for a long-term future in the company, and therefore for fulfilling its true potential.

## The problem-solving structure

The main tool of a Quality Circles programme is the problem-solving structure which is used by the groups, and it is a vital ingredient in the approach. Some companies have attempted to start up Quality Circles programmes without any training, and invariably their programmes have failed after a short time. A great strength of the approach, when tackled properly, lies in its structure, the fact that the groups solve their problems in an organised and systematic way. A sound structure raises the level of confidence of management and members alike. Without the framework of a problem-solving structure we could not be as sure of success.

Given that there is a need for a structure, many variations are possible. Experience indicates that for most Circles a framework with which to work is sufficient for their everyday needs; such a framework is provided in the training package and members' handbook associated with this book. The training covers both task and process aspects of creative group problem-solving. On the task side the techniques included are brainstorming, for generating large quantities of ideas about a subject; cause and effect diagrams and six-word diagrams, which are two methods of analysing problems; different kinds of check sheets for gathering data; and finally training in making effective management presentations. All these are gathered in a ten-step procedure, which is the subject of one of the training sessions and is recommended as the framework most likely to bring success. The ten steps are the following:

Brainstorm the list of problems.
Select the general theme out of this list.
Analyse the problem which has been selected.
Decide what facts are needed to be able to solve the problem.
Gather data about the problem.
Interpret the data that have been collected.
Devise a solution to the problem based on the facts.
Prepare and give a presentation of the solution to management.
Implement the solution if agreed by management.
Monitor the results of the solution.

This is a very powerful structure, which can facilitate the success of Circles in solving their work problems; and backing it up there is training in various important process issues which Circles need to be in control of to ensure that the group works effectively. The training session entitled 'Working together' covers group dynamics, while the one on 'Dealing with problems in the group' gives guidance for confronting and solving the difficulties any group is likely to face at some stage of its existence.

The eight training sessions in the package relate closely to the structure laid down and are designed to impart formal problem-solving skills to group members. They are not meant to inhibit flexibility, however, and, where necessary, Circles should be encouraged to adapt any part of the structure or the techniques themselves to make them fit their requirements of the moment. Any temptation not to undertake the training, though, should be firmly resisted. As was stated earlier, Quality Circles need the tools if they are to do the job well.

## Start small

For Circles to be successful in the long term it is a basic requirement that the company is willing to start with a small, low key, programme and only develop it at the pace demanded by the volunteers who come forward for future phases. There is sometimes a temptation to launch a concept on a widespread basis from the start, but this could lead to a perception that the company is merely climbing on to a short-term bandwagon rather than starting a substantial effort to encourage people to assist in making the company more effective. The benefits of starting small, with anything between two and six Circles, depending on the size of the business, are twofold. Firstly, the key principles of the approach, especially its voluntary nature, can not only be applied but be seen to be being applied, and, secondly, it gives the company the chance of adapting the approach to suit its particular circumstances. If Quality Circles are to work, they must mould themselves into the right shape to be a part of the normal way things are done in any company. The sure way to failure is to insist rigidly that the company must become 'Quality Circle shaped', since this insistence will be likely to be unacceptable to many employees, staff and management alike, and, furthermore, it will not give the concept the necessary ability to survive in the real world by adapting itself to changing circumstances.

## The right frame of mind

It has been stressed before, and will be so again, that Quality Circles will respond according to the way they are handled, and to the true motivation of the organisation in introducing the concept. Quality Circles can be introduced as a short-term management gimmick – a way of focusing attention for a short while on the need to get some problem solved at staff level, or, even more cynically, a way of manipulating staff into a belief that they are participating. We have no sympathy with these approaches, but clearly there are likely to be companies which introduce the concept with these motivations. On the other hand, Quality Circles can materially help to change the way things are done in a company by creating an environment in which everyone can and does win. The idea of win/win has been explored in depth in Chapter 3 and needs no elaboration here. There is a requirement, however, to explore briefly what win/win implies in terms of our state of mind.

To aim Quality circles at this end of the spectrum is to have high expectations both of the approach and also the ability of management and staff alike to cope with a new way of approaching work. The expectation required is that staff in general have the basic capability to help solve organisational problems. Because win/lose is so much part of our everyday lives, both in work and outside, it is not easy to separate appropriate and inappropriate instances of this attitude, and it is even harder to manage our behaviour in a way that will tend to reduce win/lose rather than maintain it. It is very easy to lapse into 'us and them' thinking of various sorts, and certainly it would be a brave man who would claim to have eradicated such behaviour or thoughts. The object is not perfection in this matter, rather an understanding of the concept, a belief in the possibility of working towards a win/win situation and a willingness to be honest with oneself about one's lapses.

## The commitment of resources

For a Circle programme to stand a chance of success, resources must be put behind it. It is vital that everyone recognises that Quality Circles represent an investment that has to be paid for – it is not free. There are a number of aspects to the cost of a programme which need to be made clear, but it is also worth pointing out that the biggest single worry that staff have at the start invariably relates to commitment. 'Will management still be behind it in six months' time?' is a question about the commitment of time. 'Will they spend any money on our solutions?' is about financial commitment. 'Will they allow us the time to meet?' questions the commitment of time to the project from the perspective of Circle members. It is important that a Quality Circle programme costs something. The willingness to pay the different prices is, as much as anything, a demonstration of the various kinds of commitment required for long-term success.

There are five main areas of resource commitment that any company wanting to introduce Quality Circles will have to consider. Firstly, there is senior management time, though experience shows that the calls on senior management time are not heavy. Circles, because they work through the normal management structure and do not miss levels out, are not constantly knocking on the managing director's door. Senior people need to spend as much time as it takes to indicate the scale of their commitment to the programme. It is more a question of communicating the intensity of their belief than spending hours attending Circle meetings and administering the programme.

The second area where commitment of resources is required is in the provision of co-ordinator and facilitator time to support the programme and to help new Circles set themselves up effectively. The cost of this aspect of resourcing depends on the way it is organised, and the view taken about costing. The usual, and best, way of providing this level of resource is as a part-time voluntary commitment to be done as well as the normal job. Experience indicates that this is a very practical and acceptable method of organising events, since it spreads the base of the programme from the start and gives a number of people the chance to join in and help. For most people the Quality Circle time requirement amounts to less than half a day a week, and it has been found that enough volunteers can so organise their affairs as to make this possible. Therefore, though there is a cost in that those taking part are not doing other things during the time they are working with Circles, it could be argued that the cost in financial terms is nil, since it is a fixed cost which would have been paid anyway. Our view, however, is that the resources allocated should be costed in financial terms, for the simple reason that if the Quality Circles themselves are encouraged to calculate the payback of their solutions, the whole programme should be subjected to the same discipline. As mentioned in Chapter 1, the average payback for a Quality Circle programme is between £5 and £8 per year for every pound invested, and any company introducing a programme should be encouraged to calculate its own investment in these terms.

The third area of resources is the time of Circle leaders

and members to hold their meetings. Quality Circles make a conscious choice to invest an hour of the working week working on and solving job-related problems, so the approach is clearly to do with work. Thus, the meetings are held in paid time, giving rise to both a time cost and a financial cost; and for the reasons outlined above the amount of the investment should be calculated to set against the benefits achieved.

The fourth area also relates to the Circle but concerns any costs arising from the solutions proposed by the groups. The thought of these costs sometimes causes concern among companies thinking about introducing the concept, but rarely among those who have had experience of what actually happens. The reasons for this are, first, that Quality Circles are given the brief of putting their own house in order, of concentrating their attention on things in their section that they can do something about, a brief that in most cases puts a natural limit on the scale of investment that might be proposed by any group. Secondly, Circles are given training in presenting data-based solutions and in calculating payback periods where required, and such training ensures that any solutions requiring an investment of money will have been checked out by the group, before presentation, in terms of their likely acceptability. Thirdly, Circles are taught that they, as well as everyone else, have to live in the real world, and that there will therefore be occasions when, for one reason or another, their solutions will not be accepted. As long as management is able to explain the reasoning behind decisions, Circle members will be able to live with them, and get on with the job of tackling either a different aspect of the problem or an entirely different problem. These safeguards help to ensure that the whole Circle programme is controlled by the usual 'laws' of investment. Management is not asked to take things on trust, it is asked to make commercial decisions based on the facts.

The fifth and final area of cost associated with Quality

Circles is the outlay required to set up the programme in the first place, which will depend largely on the requirement for external consulting assistance. The potential of Quality Circles is such that it is worth spending money at the outset where necessary, to ensure that the programme is set up soundly and that a solid framework is built. The amount required will depend on the size and complexity of the company, the availability and skill of internal resources, and the type of outside assistance sought. At an absolute minimum it will be the cost of the training materials. The maximum is not easy to quantify, since it depends entirely on the particular company and its situation. All that can be said is that if outside resources are used, they should be specialists, not only in Quality Circles but also in developing the human resource.

It can be seen then that a basic requirement for success is the willingness to commit resources of different types to the programme. World-wide experience shows conclusively that the approach is cost-effective, and so this requirement should not be too frightening; it is there, however, and needs to be recognised from the outset.

## Further reading

Osborn, Alex, F., *Applied Imagination*, Charles Scribner and Sons, New York, 1957.

Rawlinson, J. Geoffrey, *Creative Thinking and Brainstorming*, Gower, Aldershot, 1981.

Vroom, Victor, *Work and Motivation*, John Wiley & Sons, New York, 1964.

# Chapter 6

# ROLES AND RESOURCES

This chapter deals with the requirement for resources in setting up a Quality Circles programme and also the key roles involved. Furthermore, it confronts, and recommends guidelines on, the issue of the balance between using internal resources and outside consultants.

## Training

Successful Quality Circles programmes are heavily dependent on successful training, so organising the training resource is an important part of the planning of any introduction. Apart from very small businesses, most companies have training departments. It should not be taken entirely for granted, however, that where a company has a training department it has no need of any assistance in training of the kind required to introduce Quality Circles successfully. Even in some large companies the training department will only have experience of operator skills training, which is altogether different from the kind required here. The requirement is threefold: first, to train the facilitators in the skills required for that role; secondly, to train potential Circle leaders; and, thirdly, to ensure that leaders and facilitators are able to train Circle members successfully. While the programme of which this book forms a part contains detailed training material and notes to undertake this task, many trainers, both full-time professionals or part-time non-specialists, might sensibly choose to seek a limited amount of help from outside sources to see them through at least one cycle. Trainers who have been running management and supervisory courses will be more likely to feel at ease with the training requirement from the start, and may not require any outside help. Certainly a decision is required at the outset concerning the handling of the training requirement, and this book will help companies to make the correct decisions for their own circumstances.

## The co-ordinator

Every Quality Circle programme needs co-ordinating, and one of the first decisions to make is who will undertake the role. Before we discuss the kind of person required, however, we shall look at the functions of the co-ordinator. Firstly, he is required as a focal point for the programme. Although the Circles themselves are the major focus of attention, the programme itself needs someone to look after it enthusiastically, someone who is identified with it. This part of the role is important, since it gives the opportunity for people at all levels to ask questions about the programme. There will be different questions from different people, so that the co-ordinator needs to keep up to date with events and be able to see the programme through the eyes of supporters and opponents as well as at all different levels in the organisation.

The co-ordinator's second task is to administer the programme. The extent of this requirement will depend on how many Circles there are and the complexities of the particular business. Ensuring that the training material is available and not double booked, and that there is adequate cover of facilitators for holidays and sickness, are two administrative tasks, and though they might sound trivial, they are very important to the smooth running of the programme. The effective use of time is a key factor in Circle programmes, since the meetings are limited to an hour, and for time to be used well requires efficient administration. As with many similar situations the requirement is usually a diminishing one, since the groups will quickly get into the habit of meeting at a certain time on a certain day, and where this is the case, the administration tends to be standard as well. There will be the regular requirement of coping with the demands of new groups, however, and with programmes of 100 or more Circles there is often a need for a full-time co-ordinator. The administrative requirement should always, however, be kept to an absolute minimum, and the utmost care should be taken to avoid turning the programme into an unwieldy bureaucracy, since this would ensure failure in the end.

The third task of the co-ordinator is to ensure good communications between Circles, facilitators and others who are not direct participants in the programme. As far as Circles are concerned, it is always useful to set aside an hour every six to eight weeks for Circle leaders to get together to report on progress and to discuss any problems they have. Many companies also invite supervisors who have trained as Circle leaders but have not yet started a group to these meetings to keep them informed. A good deal of learning can come from such meetings if they are handled well, and it is the job of the co-ordinator to ensure that this is the case. Meetings between facilitators should take place more frequently, especially at the start of the programme and where newly trained facilitators are concerned. Such meetings should take place weekly or fortnightly and should last an hour at most; often half an hour is sufficient. Again the co-ordinator should ensure that the time is used well, and this is usually achieved by spending the time on a brief exchange of experiences since the last meeting and then focusing on one of the key dynamics emerging from the Circles and sharing views about how to tackle it within the role of facilitator. Groups tend to go through phases when different things preoccupy them and affect their work. At any stage there are likely to be a small number of key dynamics which characterise the group at that time and it is those that the facilitators should isolate and discuss, since their ability to diagnose and interpret group behaviour is as important as their skills in facilitating it.

A further vital communication need is with those who have chosen not to take part in the programme, at least for the time being. It is all too easy to forget that there is a world outside and that ultimately the success of Circles hinges on their ability to exist within it. There is no doubt that to some people Quality Circles can appear threatening at first, and it is essential for any perceived threat to be exposed as groundless. Chapter 10 deals with this issue in more depth, and so it is sufficient for now to make it clear that the co-ordinator is responsible for ensuring that Circles make it easy for others to 'buy in' to the programme. The usual way is a series of measures to establish first-class communications and a win/win frame of mind.

The fourth task which falls to the co-ordinator is to 'oil the wheels' as and when it is necessary, while being careful to ensure that any oiling does not take the ownership of the process of Circle working away from the members. It is up to Circles to decide which problem they want to work on and formulate their solutions to the best of their ability. If there are any problems outside the Circle which hinder this process, the facilitator at first, and then the co-ordinator, can help; but it will be appreciated that this must be done with discretion or both the Circle and everyone else may be alienated. The most likely difficulties here will be the unwillingness or inability of some people to make themselves available to discuss the problem or attend a presentation of the Circle's recommended solution. Fortunately this does not happen very often, but it is important to handle it correctly where it does occur.

A fifth job of the co-ordinator is to make policy decisions relating to the programme and to plan any phases of expansion. This job can include organising further presentations, getting volunteer facilitators and leaders and arranging for their training, and helping to set up the new Circles in the administrative sense. Quality Circles are very sensitive to the resources put into the programme at the start of any phase, and so the logistics of any expansion need to be thought through with considerable care.

The sixth key role of the co-ordinator is to preserve the core principles of the approach and not to allow any dilution for reasons of expediency. Quality Circles are not inflexible, far from it; to be really successful, as has already been said, the programme needs to mould itself to the needs of the company. There are certain core principles, however, which should not be violated, and it is up to the co-ordinator to ensure that they are preserved intact. Keeping to the right path is often more difficult than might appear, particularly when apparently pragmatic suggestions are put forward to change the rules. It is all too easy to end up with a programme which on analysis simply is not Quality Circles.

It is clear that the role of co-ordinator is a responsible one. It needs to be filled by someone who is in a senior enough position to have access to top management, and thus secure its continuing commitment. Furthermore, it is important that the person who fills the role has sufficient legitimate influence to be able to 'unstick' things as required. Fortunately the job does not usually take up too much time, and once the programme has been well and truly established, much of the remaining administration can be delegated. It is unwise, however, to start a programme without active senior-management support, and the role best suited for ensuring such support is certainly that of co-ordinator.

## The facilitator

The role of facilitator or Circle helper is also very important to the success of Quality Circles. It is very much a part-time and temporary job. Facilitators usually come from the ranks of middle management and are, of course, volunteers. By far the most important task of a facilitator is to make the Circle independent of him as soon as possible. This drive towards self-sufficiency is the key to the whole approach, but it is difficult to achieve unless the facilitator is clear in his own mind about the nature of the task he undertakes. It is both simple and, for some, very compelling to make the group dependent, with the result that the facilitator, rather than the group members, comes to own the Circle. Quite obviously this sort of group is likely not to stand the test of time. The trouble with this kind of facilitator behaviour is that it can develop subtly, almost to the point where it can be subconscious. Any facilitator who has a group that he is still actively busy with after six months or so should question himself, and be questioned by the co-ordinator and the other facilitators in the team, about whether he *is* making the group dependent on him. It will not necessarily be the case, but such situations demand a serious review.

The second important role of the facilitator has some bearing on whether he falls into the trap outlined above. The facilitator is not meant to be a technical resource to the Circle – someone who can solve their problems for them. It is the job of the Circles to solve their own problems. He has a vital role, however, in providing feedback about issues of group process within the group, since group process, or how the Circle goes about performing its chosen task, has a huge effect on its ultimate success.

The third important role of the facilitator is to ensure that the supervisor develops in both competence and confidence in the leadership of the group. The facilitator can help, first by assisting in a planning discussion before the Circle meeting. Here the leader and facilitator decide what the detailed agenda will be for the next Circle meeting. The facilitator then attends the meeting, and

# QUALITY CIRCLES

## the in-company training programme

. . . which is referred to in the text of this book is a comprehensive training package containing everything required to put Quality Circles into operation in your organisation.

If you would like to receive full details of this package, simply fill in and return this reply-paid card to us.

**Please send me details of the Quality Circles in-company training programme.**

Name ......................................................................................................

Position ..................................................................................................

Company ...............................................................................................

Address .................................................................................................

..............................................................................................................

..............................................................................................................

Postcode ...............................................................................

Telephone no. ......................................................................

Signed ..................................................................................

SEND FOR DETAILS
NO OBLIGATION

Do not affix Postage Stamps if posted in
Gt Britain, Channel Islands, N Ireland
or the Isle of Man

BUSINESS REPLY SERVICE
Licence No AT 170

Janet Buckingham
Gower TFI Limited
Gower House
Croft Road
Aldershot
Hampshire GU11 3HR

Postage
will be
paid by
licensee

may during the early weeks assist with some of the training. After the meeting the facilitator has a role in debriefing the leader in terms of his performance, as well as feeding back any important issues of group process. Thus the role includes that of practical supervisory developer, and, done well, it can bring truly remarkable improvements in the performance of those concerned. In line with this part of the role the facilitator should make every effort to pass the task of training over to the leader before all the training sessions have been completed, and the lead role in the planning session should also be transferred as the leader's confidence and ability develop.

A fourth aspect of the Circle helper's task must be to encourage the leader and members to make it easy for others, whether managers or staff, to support the programme. The requirement is crucial when it comes to management. There is often a tendency for criticism and win/lose to persist in the relationship between management and staff, and the Circles need to understand that the problem cannot be solved without their being willing to make it easy for management to 'buy in' to the Circle idea (see Chapter 10). Every facilitator needs to have thought about the reactions to Circles by other middle managers, and about the responses and assumptions made by Circles members in relation to management. In this way it will be possible for him to understand with more precision the nature of the win/lose situation and to be in a better position to help all parties convert it into win/win. The Circles have a primary role in achieving this, and it is for the facilitator to foster the kind of climate in which it can take place.

Fifthly, the facilitator role is likely to involve assisting with arrangements, as well as 'oiling the wheels' of progress, as necessary, without falling into the trap of doing everything himself. It is quite likely, for example, that the Circle leader will have had very little contact with

those who might need to come to a management presentation by the group, and in such circumstances it
might well be sensible for the facilitator to help in setting
up such a meeting. Equally, if a solution which has been
accepted by management gets stuck in the implementation phase, it may well be that the facilitator can help.
Both types of situation, however, should be treated as
mini-training exercises for the leader, so that there is
more chance of the Circle handling such circumstances
itself if they happen again.

The role of facilitator is not only vital in helping Quality
Circles get off the ground, it is usually felt to be very
rewarding by those who choose to take on the job. As a
rule of thumb, each Circle is likely to need up to half a
day per week of a facilitator's time for the first three
months, and then up to a quarter of a day a week for a
maximum of a further three months. By the end of the six
months the Circle should be self-sufficient, and many
groups achieve this in less time. It can be seen, therefore,
that there is no escape from the fact that time is required,
but it is not an inordinate amount, and most people who
want to have a go seem to be able to find at least the time
to look after one group. Clearly once a facilitator's Circle
or Circles have become independent, he can either take
on more groups or decide that he has had enough, for
the time being at least.

Many different kinds of people from all sorts of background make excellent facilitators. The main quality
seems to be a belief in the capacity of people in general
to solve their work problems, given the right environment and framework within which to do so, and an
interest in working with people. Thus a spell as a Circle
helper can help to develop managerial skills; and so
Quality Circles can be seen, at least in part, as a very
practical management development programme.

## The Circle leader
The Circle leader is in many ways the focal point of

Quality Circles. As the normal line supervisor of the area from which the Circle comes, he is in an ideal position to lead the group, though the role is not always an easy one. The task of the Circle leader is to run an effective problem-solving group which is basically self-sufficient, but before he can do this, he must develop the necessary skills both in himself and the Circle members. The leader needs to develop both his confidence and competence in both leading the group and in the skills of structured problem-solving. In an ideal world, of course, this would be happening already, but in fact it is unusual to find a company in which supervisory performance in these terms could not be substantially improved. It is very important to recognise that the situation in which the average supervisor finds himself is very different from the ideal, and that there is work to be done in achieving the required state of affairs. In terms of the skills of systematic problem-solving, he receives training, he has the material readily available to be reviewed at any time, and the facilitator is on hand to ensure that the first round or rounds of 'live' problems-solving go well and that the 'theoretical' skills become translated into practice.

The development of leadership skills is handled in two main ways. Firstly, the supervisor receives training in the problem-solving techniques early in the programme and then, with as much or as little assistance from the facilitator as is required, proceeds to train his members in the same subjects during the early Circle meetings. Clearly this will be a new role for many, and usually represents a combination of threat and challenge. The role of trainer is in itself an important first step in developing into the natural and knowledgeable leader of the Circle as well as the leader by virtue of position; and it is important, therefore, from all points of view that the supervisor plays at least some active role at some stage during member training, even if it is only to change the visual aids.

The second facet of the development of leader skills is

the feedback discussions held between leader and facilitator after the Circle meetings, at which both task and process issues are discussed. It is clearly necessary to review progress being made on the task at hand, but it is also essential to discuss the meeting itself, how it was handled and what were the dynamics that affected it for better or worse. Doing this as soon after the meeting as possible has the great advantage of allowing discussion of what actually happened rather than discussion of theoretical examples. Both facilitator and leader have an active role in doing this from the outset, since the ability to run successful meetings depends to a great extent on being in control of the processes of the group. Even when the group is self-sufficient, and the facilitator no longer attends the meetings, the leader should automatically spend a few minutes reviewing the meeting in terms of process and be setting himself goals for improvement of his skills in this area.

Three other key leader tasks are to ensure that the members feel comfortable in and with the group, to prevent the Circle being seen in any way as an élite club, and to administer the problem-solving activities as needed. As far as member satisfaction is concerned, the leader should ensure that no one feels threatened in any way by the training material or any other facet of the working of the group. Furthermore, there is often a requirement to handle the expectations of members, especially if they are unrealistic. Living in the real world is an important part of Quality Circles, and the world is unlikely to change overnight, however we might like it to. Simply saying this, though, does not necessarily stop the frustration that people might be experiencing, and the leader needs to be sensitive to the needs of the Circle members and to assist in the development of high but realistic expectations.

The administration of Circle work can cover a range of activities, including such matters as arranging for technical specialists or management to come to meetings as required, scheduling the collection of data relevant to the problem currently being tackled, ensuring that the meeting room will be available and setting it up ready for the Circle. It is all too easy for these details to be overlooked, and care is needed to ensure that they are handled well, since they reflect on the professionalism of the group.

The importance of avoiding any kind of élitism cannot be overstated, since élitism will invariably reduce the effectiveness of the group, and probably the section or department as well. The perception of élitism can come either from Circle members or from staff who choose not to take part, and the leader needs to act quickly to stop it. The leader can also help to prevent it happening in the first place in two main ways. Firstly, the work of the Quality Circle should not in any way be secret. It is very positively to be shared among everyone who cares to take an interest. In consequence, wherever possible, the working papers of the group should be posted up at the workplace for everyone to see and to add to if they so desire, and certainly the action minutes of the meetings should be freely available for everyone to look at. A Quality Circle is not a secret society. The second way the leader can help to stop élitism is by making it quite clear from his behaviour to both the Circle and other members of staff that there is no difference between them. A key point about voluntariness is that an equal amount of respect is due to people who volunteer or choose not to, and it is worth making this point at the outset and repeating it frequently. By carefully watching out for any hint of élitism, and by acting swiftly to confront it and stamp it out, the leader should be able to avoid the inherent dangers.

In summary, then, the role of Circle leader is to develop an effective problem-solving group and to ensure that the group fits comfortably into its environment at work.

## Outside resources

Whatever the use made of outside resources in introducing Quality Circles, it should be clear in everyone's mind from the start that, to be successful, the programme needs to become self-supporting as soon as possible, with the members running the programme on their own. Having said this, we must add that there is often a very good case for using consultants to help ensure that a solid foundation is built. If this is done, it is essential to employ a reputable consultancy, one that has had experience of helping companies introduce Quality Circles. Having run a few training courses on the subject is insufficient, since a high level of skill is required to develop the internal resources to the extent needed to manage the programme effectively. Consultancies with a track record in management and supervisory development as well as Quality Circles are, therefore, the most suitable.

Different types of company will, of course, have different levels of requirement, the specific extent of which will depend upon the availability of skilled internal resources to put behind the programme at the outset. Large companies are often characterised by organisational complexity, long lines of communication, difficult industrial relations and a tendency towards the alienation of the workforce. It is difficult to achieve the successful introduction of Quality Circles into companies of this sort, and even harder to set up the framework which gives it the chance to fulfil its true potential.

Organisational complexity is in itself sometimes a barrier to change, especially a change as fundamental as the way that the human resource is viewed by the company and its operating managers, and the way management is viewed by the workforce; and the introduction of the concept needs to be managed in the light of this knowledge. It is all too easy to set up one or two Circles in a quiet corner of the company, taste success, become over-excited, and then find that the dreamed-of expansion does not happen and that all of a sudden everyone is interested in something else. There is much work to do outside the Circle in complex environments, probably more than within the Circles themselves, and to be successful in any but the short term requires considerable knowledge and skills at dealing with large-scale organisational change. Quality Circles ultimately are affected by, and have an effect on, the whole organisation, in that they become part of the way things are done. To get to this stage takes a long time and much skill, care and knowledge of the way both organisations and people work.

In terms of an introductory programme, therefore, a large organisation should, first of all, assess the availability of internal resources capable of handling the effort, and, secondly, decide whether it can provide the training expertise required from the start or whether internal resources capable of handling both sets of tasks will need to be developed. If the company believes it has the requisite level of skills available, the programme of which this book is a part will enable it to manage its own programme from the start. If not, external resources should be selectively employed, on the clear understanding that their role is developmental. No programme will be successful in the long run unless it is entirely owned and run by internal resources.

Medium-sized companies are likely to be rather less complex in organisational terms than large ones, which is not to imply that the introduction of Quality Circles will be simple. Lines of communication, although shorter, are still likely to be long enough to cause problems, and industrial relations, if not an actual problem, may be a potential one. The kinds of resource required for introducing Quality Circles into medium-sized companies are, in essence, the same as for large ones: one, ability to cope with and manage organisational change, and two, expertise in training. The extent of any outside assistance needed in the organisational change aspect should of course reflect the complexity of the business – the less complex, the less help is likely to be required.

Small companies will probably have fewer problems of communication, since there are likely to be fewer levels of staff, and the better the communications, the easier it is for Quality Circles to fulfil their potential. The problem small companies have, however, is that often there are few staff specialists, such as trainers, available. In such cases the material associated with this book provides an invaluable framework, which can be backed up if necessary by selective use of consultancy inputs, probably to develop an appropriate competence in training.

It has often been said that a company only has one chance to introduce Quality Circles, and that if the opportunity is wasted, it has gone, if not forever, certainly for a considerable time. All of this argues for a careful and honest assessment of internal capability as part of the decision whether or not to call on outside assistance at the start. There is no point in using consultants if the capability is available and developed in house; equally, if they are to be used, it must be to develop internal resources. As we have said, the consultants who have a credible track record in people development as well as Quality Circles are likely to be of most assistance to a company, whatever its size. In large companies an additional requirement for the consultants should be experience in handling large-scale organisational change.

In summary, then, the decision about resourcing at the start of the programme depends on the internal availability of the required quantity and quality of staff, and on the company's attitude to using consultants. The implementation package of which this book forms the first part can materially assist, whichever way the company decides to resource its programme.

# Chapter 7

# THE PROGRAMME OF INTRODUCTION

This chapter deals with the mechanics of introducing Quality Circles into a company. The precise order of the stages may vary slightly in different organisational settings, and in some circumstances it may be possible and desirable to deal with some stages in parallel; the programme as laid out, therefore, should be seen as a flexible model to be adapted to suit the requirement of the company concerned.

It has been assumed that the company has the skilled resources available to tackle the introduction. Were outside resources to be used, the programme would remain basically the same, with the specialist skills being 'plugged in' at the appropriate places.

## Selecting the co-ordinator

The role of the co-ordinator has been discussed in some detail in the previous chapter. The best person for the job is probably a senior manager, since the co-ordinator must have ready access to top management to maintain its commitment, and, indeed, to act as a demonstration of that commitment. It is also sensible to have someone in this role who has enough legitimate influence to be able to deal with the occasional impasse, and to ensure that the programme runs smoothly in an administrative sense.

In many companies there will be a natural choice – maybe the person whose enthusiasm and influence were instrumental in the agreement to introduce Quality

Circles, or someone whose central position and interest in the concept makes him or her the logical contender. The appointment needs to be made at the beginning of the programme, for there is much to do.

## How many Circles to start with?

An early decision, to be made by the co-ordinator in conjunction with the managing director and other nominated top managers, is the number of Quality Circles that should be the initial aim of the company. An important basic requirement is that the organisation is prepared to go slowly, especially at first, and to develop in line with the extent of enthusiasm and commitment among managers and staff alike. The appropriate number of Circles to begin with depends, in addition, on the size of the company; but whatever the size, above the very smallest business, it is sensible to start with more than one group. Starting with just one Circle may appear attractive in some situations, since it could be felt that doing so would minimise the risks while allowing the approach to prove its value. The reasons for believing a one-Circle pilot scheme to be unwise are pragmatic rather than philosophical. Starting with one group puts all the eggs into one basket, and leads to the temptation for interested parties to 'make' it work. If this temptation is succumbed to, a fundamental weakness has been built in from the start for, amongst other things, being the only group is very likely to put a degree of pressure on the members which could very easily threaten the principle of voluntariness that is so crucial to success. A further weakness of starting with one Circle is that the data base for a go/no go decision after phase one would be too small and too narrow.

Even a small company, therefore, should aim at setting up two Circles to begin with. In a medium-sized company the recommended number is four, and in a large one six. This gives the programme a broad enough base from the beginning. It prevents any single Circle feeling that the responsibility for the success of the whole of the programme rests with it alone, and it also provides a stronger base for extending the scheme. To start these numbers of Circles, however, will not commit the company to the approach before it has proved its worth. To start six Circles is only likely to involve about fifty or sixty people, which is only a very small proportion of a large company. The first introduction can, therefore, be a genuine pilot study to test the approach and to gather sufficient data to enable a decision to be made about expansion.

A decision on the number of Circles must be followed by a decision about which parts of the company they should come from. It is not unusual for people to fall into the trap of specifying the precise areas in which Circles will be formed, quite forgetting that whether or not that happens depends on who volunteers. In stating that a decision is required about which parts of the company Circles should come from, therefore, we mean whether everyone in the company or division will be given the chance to come forward or whether the pilot study will be limited to certain departments. There are sometimes good reasons for limiting the opportunity to volunteer at the first stage, but as a general rule it is advisable to spread the base wide right from the start. Circles are relevant in offices, workshops and production areas, and to include all departments from the start makes for a genuinely broad-based experiment. A further reason for taking this approach is that, as Circles become mature, they often begin working with each other to solve problems at the interface of their departments, and it is as well to build this opportunity in from the beginning.

## Communication

Full and effective communication is an absolute essential of the introduction of Quality Circles. Even if the pilot scheme is to be limited to specific areas, everyone in the company or division should be informed of what is happening and of the reasons why. The method of communication should comprise meetings and a handout. Firstly, meetings should be arranged to cover all management, down to and including first-line supervision, and senior trade union officials, in groups of up to twenty or so. It is usually advisable to hold the union meeting separately to avoid the danger of Quality Circles getting tangled up in other issues at the start, but the content of this meeting should be exactly the same as that for management.

The basic format of the meeting should be a presentation lasting for half an hour, followed by an hour of questions and discussion. The purpose of the meetings is to tell management and unions what Quality Circles are, the principles of the approach and the company's plan for introducing them. A tried and tested agenda includes the following items:

1   A statement that the company wants to introduce Quality Circles and that these meetings are designed to start the programme off and let everyone know what is happening.
2   A statement about the centrality of management to the whole concept. This topic is covered fully in Chapter 10, and it should be read up and thought about deeply before the presentation.
3   The background and history of the approach.
4   A definition of Quality Circles in broad terms.
5   A clear statement of the key principles of voluntariness at all levels, and an explanation that no Quality Circles will be formed in the department of a manager who does not want them.
6   Who takes part in Quality Circles, how often they meet and what they do in the meetings.
7   The fact that meetings are held in paid time.

8   An outline of the training which will be given to Circle leaders and members, including an overview of the problem-solving techniques.
9   A brief outline of the role of the facilitator.
10  A statement of the company's objectives in wanting to start Quality Circles.
11  The benefits to management, supervisors and Circle members.
12  The number of Circles it is hoped to start in the first phase, and the reasons for starting with a small pilot scheme.
13  The level of commitment of top management to the concept.
14  An outline of the proposed programme.
15  An invitation to first-line supervisors to volunteer to go on the leader's training course, and a statement that at the end of the course attendees will be asked if they want to volunteer to set up a Circle.
16  An invitation to middle managers to volunteer to be trained as facilitators.
17  An invitation to ask questions.

Since this will be the first time many people have come into contact with the concept of Quality Circles, it is obviously important that the presentation is well prepared and backed up with good visual aids. In the training package associated with this book the first of the training sessions contains an introduction to the approach and so if required can be adapted or used in full for these introductory talks. However these presentations are organised, they should be backed up with a written handout which summarises the key principles. This document should be made available not only to management and unions but also to all employees. A typical brochure would consist of the following information:

1   Introduction.
    An introduction to the company and the requirements

(e.g. for high quality) that led to the decision to introduce Quality Circles.

2   Quality Circles can help to achieve these objectives by making better use of the knowledge and creativity of the people doing the job.

3   A Quality Circle is a group of four to ten people from the same work group who volunteer to start a Circle. Each week they meet under the leadership of their supervisor, who is also a volunteer. At the meeting, which lasts for an hour and is held in normal working hours, they identify and analyse problems related to their own work area. Having done this, they devise a solution and present their proposals to management for a decision. If approved, the solution is implemented by the Circle or by management as appropriate.

4   Quality Circles are entirely voluntary, no pressure is put on anyone to join in, and there are no penalties against anyone who prefers not to take part.

5   Experience shows that it is best to start small and to expand the programme gradually. With this in mind we plan to start up to $x$ Circles to begin with and to increase the number progressively so that ultimately everyone will have a chance to join a Circle.

6   In summary then:

*What is a Quality Circle?*

It is a group of four to ten volunteers who:

(a)  work in the same section;

(b)  meet weekly for an hour;

(c)  identify, analyse and solve their own work-related problems.

*How do they become effective?*

Circle leaders and members receive special training in:

(a)  problem analysis;

(b)  problem-solving methods;

(c)  presentation of their findings.

*Where can Quality Circles be used?*
(a) Quality Circles are applicable to virtually any work area, department or section in the business.
(b) Anyone who is interested can use it.
*What's in it for you?*
The opportunity to:
(a) tackle the problems which matter to you;
(b) have a say in what is done about them;
(c) make your point of view known;
(d) get things done;
(e) receive training to help you.
*How does the company gain?*
Better quality of work leads to:
(a) less wastage;
(b) reduced costs;
(c) improved service.

In the long run these will help us to become a more successful company.

An attractively produced brochure containing this information will ensure that all employees know what is happening. In small companies it may be possible to achieve this without the formality of the written word, but whichever method is chosen, it is vital that everyone be given the opportunity of knowing what Quality Circles are and the company's plan for introducing them.

## The volunteers for the leader course

As we have seen, a part of the initial presentations made to first-line supervisors should be to invite them to put their names forward for the leader training course. This does not commit them to starting a Circle; indeed, it is only at the end of the course that anyone will be invited to volunteer to start up a group.

The right number of supervisors to have on the leader course depends on the number of Circles the company wishes to get going in stage one. Clearly since the process of voluntariness is a two-stage one, the supervisors to be trained should outnumber the Circles it is intended to start, but not by so many more that anyone wanting to start a group cannot look ahead to the time when he or she will be able to do so. As a rule of thumb, then, the number of supervisors trained in the first course should be double the number of Circles it is intended to start with. No one will then come under pressure to volunteer, but enough will probably volunteer to get the programme off the ground.

One potential problem is that more supervisors might volunteer than there are places on the course. The best way of handling this situation is to establish a set of logical principles which will govern the selection of the first group to be trained. A key criterion is likely to be the spread of departments represented, to give the pilot study a broad base. Once the principles are established and the selection made on this basis, each person who is not on the list should be seen individually and informed of the criteria used and thus the reasons for not including him or her in the first course. It should be made quite clear that no one is being excluded totally, and that when the next course is run, the initial volunteers will be the first to be approached. To be able to give an estimate of when the next course is likely to be run, if all goes well, is often helpful, since it gives a positive expectation of being trained in the not too distant future. An excess of volunteers can create a difficult situation, and the way to deal with it should be thought out very carefully before anyone is spoken to, since to cause any bad feeling at this stage would be most unfortunate.

## Checking management opinions

It is important to check the management structure above the volunteers to ensure that there are no managers who have a fundamental objection to the concept being operated within their span of control. This point has already been emphasised in the initial presentation and must be checked out when choosing supervisors for training. Although active support and commitment are desirable, they are not essential at the beginning. A willingness to allow the experiment is, in some circumstances, all that can reasonably be expected, and experience shows that initial willingness usually converts itself into active support on the basis of Circle achievements over six to nine months.

Circles should not be started in areas where there is a positive objection, and it is unwise to raise the expectations of supervisors from these areas by letting them come on the course. Every attempt must be made, however, to ensure that no acrimony remains, and that the door is left very much open for anyone to join in at a later stage. There is no doubt that different people come to support Quality Circles at different times, and some never do. A key point about voluntariness is that it does not require people to change their minds at anything other than their own natural pace.

## The volunteer facilitators

As part of the initial presentations managers will have been invited to volunteer for the role of facilitator. The number required will clearly depend on the number of Circles to be started, on the one hand, and the time that volunteers have available, on the other. It has already been established as a rule of thumb that a maximum of a half a day of facilitator time per Circle per week will be required for the first three months or so, and a quarter of a day per Circle per week for up to another three months. This amount of support should lead to the self-sufficiency of the Circle. It is usually sensible to have more than one facilitator from the start, since this is another way of spreading the base of the programme and ensuring that not too many eggs are put into one basket. Furthermore, it allows the voluntary principle to operate in as genuine a sense with this role as it does in all other tasks associated with Quality Circles. Apart from having a high degree of usefulness in helping Quality Circles, the facilitator training represents a valuable opportunity for teaching about issues that are relevant and important to the normal line role of any manager, whose job entails getting things done through people.

As a general rule it is best to arrange that there is one facilitator per Circle, since this avoids putting too much pressure on the time of any one person. More potential facilitators than the number required immediately can be trained, since they will be a useful addition to the resource and it will avoid the need for another training programme before the launch of more Circles in phase two.

Up to the normal limits of running a course there is no limit to the number of facilitators who can be trained. In some ways, the more the merrier. But it should be made quite clear from the outset, first, the number of people who will be required in phase one, and, second, that the whole group will participate in making the decision about who they should be at the end of the training course if there are more volunteers than people required. This mechanism, although it may sound a trifle anarchistic, works very well and ensures a high degree of ownership of the decisions among the whole group, which in its turn helps to ensure the willingness of those excluded in the first phase to join in the expansion of the programme as and when it takes place.

## Facilitator training

The content of facilitator training is covered in more detail in Chapter 8, and this section is intended to indicate its place in the introductory programme and to discuss different ways of tackling it. Although the development of facilitatory skills is likely to happen primarily as a result of actual experience with Circles, it is necessary to begin the process with an induction into the role, ensuring that there is an adequate knowledge base concerning the way that Circles work, and, very importantly, spelling out the key factors which are likely to affect the development of a successful group.

There are two main ways of organising the training, and the choice will depend on the precise situation in the business. The first way is to run a full-scale course, and the second is to split up the training into a number of discrete modules and to tackle them over a period of time. The fewer facilitators being trained, the more likely it will be that the second option is appropriate; and the same will apply in situations where it proves impossible to find a number of days to take the participants away from their main line jobs.

Whether the training is done as separate modules or as a complete course matters not nearly as much as that it is done well. The success of Circles in the long run will depend to a large extent on the use to which facilitators put this early training. The role requires behaviour quite different from that often needed in the normal line manager's job, and a failure to distinguish the particular requirements for facilitating Circles has caused pro-grammes to be set up with fundamental weaknesses, such as dependency on the facilitator, built in from the start. It is obviously vital, therefore, that the trainer thoroughly understand the role and the behaviour appropriate to it.

## Leader training

Leader training is covered in detail in Chapter 9, but this section is included to indicate the stage of the introductory programme at which the need should be addressed. As with facilitator training, there is a choice to be made as to whether the training should be conducted as an integrated course or as separate modules. In most cases it will be more appropriate to run a full course, since it better enables potential leaders to see the approach, and the problem-solving techniques as a whole rather than as a collection of disparate parts.

It has already been suggested that double the number of supervisors are trained than the number of Circles to be started initially, and the facilitators who will help Circles in phase one should attend the course as well. This will give them another opportunity to become comfortable with the material, and will begin to develop their facilitative skills; furthermore, they will be able to meet and get used to the potential leaders, and vice versa.

## Selecting Circle leaders for phase 1

Double the number of leaders will have been trained than are initially required, so that, as a final part of the course, there will be a need to decide who will actually start Circles. The first stage of this process is to ask for volunteers who want to start their own group. If the course has gone well, it is likely that most people will come forward, so there is often a selection job to be done. This should be handled in much the same way as the equivalent situation with facilitators. First of all, the group should be reminded that the initial pilot scheme calls for the introduction of a particular number of Circles. The reasons for allowing more than the required number of supervisors on the course should then be repeated, together with a statement that everyone should participate in making the decision. The group should then decide on the criteria to be used in selecting the areas in which to start Circles in phase one, and from this the supervisors concerned. Many groups allocate back-up roles for other supervisors, so that they can keep in touch with progress, and agree to meet for an hour every six to eight weeks to keep everyone abreast of developments – a useful procedure in larger companies but perhaps not as necessary in smaller ones. Whatever is decided, it is wise to ensure that the trained leaders are kept interested and 'on the boil', ready for them to start their own Circles in phase two, which is usually three or four months later.

An important subsidiary point to be made about the choice of areas for Circles to start up in is that if management has a view about this it is quite valid for it to be discussed along with any other opinions. Thus, the opportunity to influence where the programme starts is available if this is deemed to be necessary. What must not be done of course is to 'send' people on the course, since this clearly violates the principle of voluntariness and such a violation will always come back to haunt the programme.

## Inducting management

The vital role that management plays in a successful Quality Circles programme is dealt with fully in Chapter 10. It is important at an early stage to give managers, especially those in areas where supervisors have volunteered to start Circles, the chance of seeing the training material and getting a deeper understanding of the concept. A meeting should be held for this purpose.

Firstly, at the meeting, it will be as well to go through the concept of Quality Circles again to make sure that the managers concerned are clear about what it entails. Probably the best way of doing this will be to go through the introductory tape, since this will give them an idea of the form of the training material, as well as reminding them of the details of the approach.

The second subject to be covered should be the training material and back-up resources to the launch. Certainly everyone should be given the opportunity of looking through the training material and the Quality Circle members' handbook, and ideally each manager should receive a copy of the book so that he can study the problem-solving techniques for himself. It is often worthwhile running through one of the other tapes as well, to give the managers an insight into how a more 'technical' subject is handled.

The third topic it will be useful to discuss concerns the prevailing attitudes among the managers regarding the start-up of Circles in their areas. There are likely to be a range of views expressed here, from the sceptical to the enthusiastic, and it will be as well to have the different opinions explicit rather than hidden away. Any sceptics can then be encouraged to keep as open a mind as possible, and perhaps to support the Circle in their area and give it a real chance. It is often appropriate to make the point that Circles can be instrumental in freeing management time, because, by working on the problems of their workplace, the Circle members can reduce the need for the manager to solve their problems for them.

Fourthly, there is a need to discuss what management can do to help Circles. The main methods are encouragment and support, and most managers find it very useful to attend the first ten minutes of a Circle meeting every three or four weeks to keep in touch with progress, and to ensure good communication. They should, of course, only attend by invitation of the Circle itself, but most Circles are delighted that their manager shows enough interest to want to come along on this basis.

Depending on how much of the training material the managers want to go through, the explanatory meeting mentioned earlier should be scheduled for two to three hours, and it should be suggested at the end of the session that periodic review meetings should be held to keep in touch with progress. These should take place every six weeks or so and should last an hour. They are a vital part of developing managerial commitment to the concept.

To fulfil its full potential the Quality Circle concept has to be accepted as an integral part of the way things are done in the company. Reaching this situation can often take a long time and can require much careful and skilful work on the part of those taking part in the programme, from Circle members to the programme co-ordinator. It should never be forgotten that Circles cannot achieve their full status unless managers 'buy in' to the concept and come to feel that managing in this way serves every-one's best interest.

## Preparing for Circle meetings

Any meeting, if it is to achieve its objective efficiently, requires preparation, and preparation is especially important in early Circle meetings, since many of the members, perhaps the leader as well, may not have much experience of attending meetings and making them work. To go into a Circle meeting inadequately prepared is to risk the very existence of the group, and to show little respect for the time that people have chosen to invest in an attempt to get things done.

The preparation for the meeting is best done between the facilitator and the leader in the early days, and up to an hour can be usefully spent preparing the first few meetings. This amount of time reduces as the skill of the leader develops, until, after three or four months, it usually takes no longer than fifteen minutes to prepare the meeting. The subject of preparation for Circle meet-ings is covered fully in Chapter 8 as a part of the recom-mended training programme for facilitators.

## Presenting to potential members

The first of the audio tapes in the training package is an introduction to Quality Circles, designed to explain what they are all about and to give sufficient background for people to be able to make up their minds whether or not they want to join in to start with. It is recommended, therefore, that the tape be used to introduce the idea to the section concerned. The procedure outlined above should be used in preparing the meeting, which should last one hour. The keynote of the session should be encouragement, but not pressure, to join. Unless there is a desire within the group to agree there and then, people should be given a few days to think it all over before deciding and putting their names forward to the supervisor.

## Running the Circle meetings

It is not intended to focus too much attention here on the skills of running effective meetings, rather to make a number of more general points that seem particularly relevant to Quality Circle meetings.

The first concerns the role of the facilitator. If the facilitator is doing the job correctly, there will be occasions, possibly many occasions, when he will not say a single word in the meeting itself, apart from the obvious pleasantries of 'hello' and 'goodbye'. Such quietness does not mean that no work is being done; indeed, quite the reverse. It is difficult and tiring to study how a group is working and to try to isolate the key dynamics of the meeting. It is, though, unusual to have someone sitting in on the meeting but, in general, playing no active role; and it is important in the first meeting that the facilitator role is made clear to everyone.

The second point worth making about Circle meetings is that the time when they meet is important, since many of the people in the groups will come from work areas where scheduling is required and where other people in the same work group can be affected if care is not taken. It has been demonstrated on many occasions that the members of the Circle itself are in the best position to decide when to meet, and experience shows that they do so to minimise the effect on output. It is usually best to have a regular arrangement of 'same time, same place, next week'.

The third point to be made about Circle meetings is that, once they get started, requests are likely to be received to 'sit in on one to see what is happening'. Quality Circle members, however, are not goldfish, and to be put on display can be distracting and annoying. This is not to say that no one should ever sit in, but serious thought should be taken before agreeing to it. This is an important issue, since many people who do not really understand Circles are nonetheless fascinated by them as a phenomenon. It is all too easy to assume that by granting such requests on a regular basis one is automatically promoting the best interests of the programme. This may be so on many occasions, but it is not necessarily the case, so caution, not inflexibility, is required.

## Reviewing Circle meetings
At the end of every Circle meeting the facilitator and leader should spend some time together reviewing what happened and why. Every effort should be made to hold the meeting immediately after the Circle while memories are still fresh. This meeting is the main opportunity the facilitator has for developing the leader, by praising what was done well and reviewing or working on those aspects capable of improvement. Review meetings are covered fully in Chapter 8.

## Minutes of Circle meetings
Circles must not become bogged down in too much formality and red tape, since this can only serve to frustrate everyone and prevent any action. It is vital, however, that the managers of the departments where there are Circles are kept informed of how the groups are using their time, and what progress they are making. Any members of sections who have chosen not to take part should also have the opportunity of seeing what the Circle is doing. Furthermore, it is useful for the group itself to have some record of its work and decisions. A standard one-page action minute statement should be devised and a copy filled in by every Circle after its meeting. The information

required is very basic: for example, the problem being worked on, the stage reached by the group and any actions agreed, including who is to perform them and by when.

A copy of the form should be posted in the workplace wherever possible, one should be sent to the supervisor's boss, and one to the co-ordinator. The form can be filled in either by the leader or a Circle member, but it must be done after every meeting, since it is vital for the work of Circles to be openly communicated to management and the rest of the section.

## When to use the training tapes

The decision when to use the training tapes is an important one, because it is essential to avoid the trap that too much training falls into, of failing to build an adequate bridge from the apparently straightforward theory of the classroom to the difficulties and problems of the real world. A simple rule should be abided by wherever possible: that any training should be reinforced immediately by putting it within a practical context. Training in brainstorming or anything else should not be given until the group is ready to use the technique and the reinforcement should take place within the same meeting. The lesson plans are structured in this way; it is a tried and tested procedure, and it should be adhered to wherever possible.

Some Quality Circles programmes have sent people to technical colleges to be trained. Others have trained up members in full-scale training courses. While either of these options is better than doing no training at all, neither is as satisfactory as being able to conduct the training within the Circle meetings, and follow it up by putting the particular technique into practice during the same meeting.

## Making sure the training sticks

Since the ultimate goal of all the training and back-up resource is to help Circles to establish themselves as self-supporting units, it is obviously important that the training sticks, and that both the confidence and competence of the group improve in terms of its ability and willingness to tackle its problems. One way of remembering what one has learned is by revision. Each Circle member will, of course, have been given a copy of the members' handbook at the start of the first full meeting of his group, and so it is always possible for him to read through the techniques at will. A second aspect of revision is that the company will have all the training material readily available, so that Circles can choose to spend time going through one or more lessons again, if they so desire. Clearly, though, the best way to learn is by using the techniques to help solve real problems. Everyone will then understand how the mechanisms work, especially if, before each time the particular technique is used, the group spends a few minutes reviewing the key rules, writing them on the flip chart and posting them up in the room somewhere so that everyone can see them.

The training that needs to stick does not only consist of the problem-solving techniques, however, for without some understanding of the underlying philosophy a technique can be rather a blunt instrument. Time is spent in the training sessions introducing and reinforcing principles of the approach, and these need to be underlined in practice, in the effort to work towards the eradication of 'us and them' attitudes, finger-pointing, and focusing on everyone else's problems.

Since it is unrealistic, and unreasonable, to expect that everyone will immediately change his behaviour as a result of the training, a mechanism is required to encourage people progressively to take the lessons on board – one that can be used is to reinforce successive approximations positively. What this assumes is that people are often unlikely to get things entirely right the first time they try it; indeed, the path to the goal might be a long and tricky one, with many instances of 'three steps forward, two steps back' on the way. To sustain effort towards the goal we require encouragement and positive feedback, which can be given during or straight after any of the 'three steps forward' stages of our behaviour. Such encouragement reinforces the principles we are attempting to build in and will help to make them second nature. The reinforcement should be specific, and aimed at the particular instances of the desired behaviour, for it is just as easy to reinforce the wrong behaviour as the desired one. Take the story of the lady who was attempting to house-train her Labrador pup. Every time the dog fouled the carpet, it was whacked with a newspaper, dragged to the door and pushed out into the garden. It very soon developed what it thought to be the desired behaviour. After it had relieved itself, it rushed to the door, panting to be let out!

The importance of receiving positive feedback cannot be over-emphasised; it is a pressing need in the vast majority of the population. What the principle of positively reinforcing successive approximations tells us is that the feedback should not be given at random, but should be directed at particular examples of behaviour which indicate that the individuals or group are getting nearer the desired state.

An important role of the facilitator and the leader in the first few months of the Circle's existence is to make the problem-solving techniques and the underlying philosophy of the approach a normal part of the way things are done. The success of the group in the longer run will depend quite considerably on this being achieved. It is not an easy task, but it is eminently achievable if tackled with thought, care and skill.

## Avoiding élitism

Avoiding élitism has been mentioned before, but is worth repeating. If élitism does creep in, it means death for that group, and maybe for the whole programme. As we have seen, the Circle leader has an important role in preventing its happening in the first place, by preventing the conditions that can lead to it from arising, or in stamping it out firmly and quickly if it does appear. It is also the shared responsibility of everyone else who is committed to the approach, to ensure that it does not happen; and the best way of doing this is to make the work of the Circle public property, and to stress that everyone can make a contribution whether they are in the group or not.

## How much pressure to put on

The dynamics of a Circle programme, especially in its early stages, are held in a delicate balance. Both management and the Circle need early results, yet the problems must be solved in a thorough and professional way, which takes time. Some Circle members will be very impatient, while some of the management may be conscious of the need to ensure that the training lessons are absorbed, again something which takes time. Management may be impatient for the Circle to choose the problem it sees as crucial, and the Circle may only have it second on its list of priorities. And so it goes on. We have seen many times that the Circles' apparent simplicity is deceptive.

The dimension it is crucial to get right concerns the degree of pressure put on the Circle by the programme through the co-ordinator and facilitator. Quite naturally, as has been said, everyone taking part in the programme will want early results to prove the concept and also help justify deciding to join. Such a desire perfectly acceptable as long as it is managed carefully, and none of the vital principles of the approach are violated.

In the early stages the Circle is unlikely to have formed itself into a fully effective group, and yet it may well be hungry for results. Some members will want to change the world overnight, and their arguments will probably be based on opinion, not facts. The disciplines so important to good group working are unlikely to be fully in force, and the leader is unlikely to be fully confident in his role. This is the background against which the leader and the facilitator must work. They can be sure that some positive outcome is required by the group, if no one else, within a fairly short space of time; consequently it is all too easy for them to make sure that something happens by doing it themselves, either obviously and openly, or, more likely, by 'feeding' answers and manipulating the situation. While this may give the Circle some sense of achievement in the short term, it also begins to set up expectations of how problems are solved and who solves them. It also leads to dependency. If this happens, the Circle is probably doomed.

The group must solve its own problems. The leader, as a member of the group, has an important role to play, but needs at the same time, with the support of the facilitator, to focus the attention of the Circle members on the core principles of the Quality Circle approach, which were discussed in Chapter 3. The need for everyone to live with the realities of the world should be stressed, and the fact that there are no wholly successful short cuts. The really important thing is that the group gets into the habit of solving its own problems in a complete and professional way, and does so as soon as possible.

## Co-ordinator meetings

As the programme gets under way, it usually becomes advisable for the co-ordinator to get together with the facilitator(s) for half an hour each week to review progress, share problems and make any forward plans that may be necessary. The precise agenda will vary with the stage of the programme and particular circumstances, and so it is not sensible to go into any more detail here. It is an important meeting, however, since it represents the chance for the co-ordinator to review the whole programme with the facilitator(s) as well as discussing each Circle. It keeps the co-ordinator fully in the picture and gives the facilitator(s) the opportunity of comparing notes and 'picking each other's brains'.

Every eight weeks or so it is invariably beneficial to widen the scope of the meeting somewhat and to invite Circle leaders along, and also supervisors who have been trained and who are waiting to start their own groups. This meeting should be scheduled to last an hour and should consist of an update on each Circle's progress, given by the leader, a discussion about any problems being experienced, and any information concerning the expansion of the programme. Such meetings ensure that all interested parties are kept abreast of developments and that any general problems can be identified and tackled before they become too serious.

# Chapter 8

# TRAINING THE FACILITATORS

The primary task of the facilitator is to develop the Circle leader and the group into self-sufficiency as soon as possible. Anyone's chance of achieving this within a reasonable time will depend partly on the ability of the particular group and partly upon his own skills in the role. The task of facilitator calls for different abilities from those normally employed in group working, and from those used in 'traditional' man management, and some induction and training, therefore, are needed for those who volunteer for the task. The dangers of unskilled facilitation are serious, and include, ultimately, the demise of the Circle; so the training requirement is a serious one.

Wherever possible, more than one facilitator should be trained, not only to provide breadth and flexibility to the programme, but also to make for a better quality of discussion during the training period. A formal training course will often be the appropriate mechanism for this task. Sometimes a series of meetings to discuss material which has been read by the participants is the best framework to use. In general, the training should be organised and carried out by the training manager, or whoever undertakes the leader training. If outside consultants are used, it is a task which can often be handled effectively by them, assuming they have the requisite knowledge about facilitation and group working to pass on. For the purpose of this chapter, however, it will be assumed that the requirement will be handled internally, and the remainder of this chapter outlines a suitable training programme and lists the specialised reading material required to enable the role to be discussed intelligently.

## The training framework

The recommended training framework is a series of six meetings, each lasting two to two and a half hours, to review the training package and to discuss other material which has already been read. The meetings can be held over any reasonable period of time, the most usual frequency being one or two per week. Up to two hours of reading will be required to get the best out of the discussions, and the programme should be planned realistically, so that the reading does get done, or else the discussions are likely to be less than satisfactory.

The audio tapes, which form a key part of the training package for Circle members, should be played and reviewed at the meetings, and the facilitators should take it in turn to lead this part of the meetings. In that way everyone will be given the opportunity for 'hands on' experience of using the training material. It will probably not be necessary to go through the discussion parts of the lesson plans in their entirety, but the recommended procedure in the lessons should be observed, so that facilitators get a real feel for the way the subjects are treated, including the timings.

## Structure of meetings

There is a lot to be accomplished at each of the facilitator training sessions and it is, therefore, important to structure them carefully.

It will usually be sensible to begin the meetings by playing the training tape or tapes. It is an important part of the training that the facilitators get the chance not only to review the material but also to get an idea of what it is like to use it. This will make them more sensitive to the feelings of Circle leaders when they are training Circle members, and will help to ensure that the feedback given about the way the training was handled is sensitive.

After the particular tape has been played, the lesson should be discussed in terms of content, and the structure of the session – for example, the positioning of the break points in the tape and the suggested activities during the breaks. Finally the facilitator who handled the session should receive feedback about his or her performance from the rest of the group.

The rest of the meeting should be spent reviewing and discussing the material which has been read in preparation for the meeting. This discussion is usually best led by the trainer, but in some circumstances it is a good idea to have a facilitator take the lead in these sessions, remembering that the facilitator role represents an opportunity to develop management skills. When it comes to the sessions where the facilitator role is discussed in detail, it will be necessary to have someone leading the discussion who understands group process in some depth.

Finally, in terms of the structure of the meetings, they should not be allowed to overrun the allotted time. If more than one meeting is needed to discuss any topic, a follow-up session should be arranged. This plan is much better than letting two and a half hour meetings drag out into three and a half hour ones. If, on the other hand, the subject under discussion has received a full and satisfactory airing in less than the time allowed, the meeting should be brought to a close early and the group should feel that it has done well. One of the key disciplines of Quality Circles is in the use of time, and facilitators need to get into the habit of thinking of this from the start. The time required to discuss a subject in the appropriate depth will depend not only on the topic itself but on the size of the group (and, therefore, the number of opinions to be taken into consideration), and also the particular interests, background and experience of group members.

## The facilitator training meetings
The six facilitator training meetings should be structured as follows.

### Meeting 1

*Preparatory reading*

This book, Chapter 1   Introduction
         Chapter 2   Development of Quality Circles
         Chapter 3   The core principles
         Chapter 4   Why bother?

Members' handbook, Session 1   An introduction to Quality Circles.

*The meeting*

1  Introduce the session by welcoming the volunteers. Key points to highlight are that the programme of induction and training consists of six sessions such as this and that the idea is to give everyone enough basic understanding of, and training in, Quality Circles and the facilitator role to enable people to make up their minds whether or not to 'sign on', and to be able to undertake the role successfully if they decide so to do.
2  The outline of the programme should be discussed, and a basic agreement as to the frequency of the meetings reached, subject to experience indicating that more meetings are required to cover the material successfully. It is useful to have a prepared handout scheduling the meetings, so that participants can see the shape of the programme clearly.
3  Introduce the training package and hand out copies of

the members' handbook for each person to keep. Outline the purpose of the two different volumes and how it is envisaged they will be used.

4   Indicate that after the introductory tape, which will be handled by the trainer, the participants will take it in turn to lead this part of the meeting, so that everyone will get a feel for the training material. State that this will require some additional preparation before the meeting.

5   Play the first tape, 'An introduction to Quality Circles'. In doing so, use the break points in the lesson and indicate that this is what should be done in subsequent sessions.

6   Review the material, the visual aids and the lesson plan itself in terms of what needs to be achieved in the introductory meeting for a work group to learn about Quality Circles, and give enough information to enable people to decide whether or not they wish to volunteer.

7   Move the meeting on to a discussion of the preparatory reading. Among the topics which it is vital to cover are:

(a)  The goals of the Quality Circle programme in the company.

(b)  What is the potential of the approach in this environment?

(c)  Which of the core principles are likely to be the most difficult to get operating?

(d)  The difficulty of achieving a win/win situation, and the importance of working towards this outcome.

It will often be appropriate, and may result in a better quality of discussion, if some of the key topics are allocated to individual volunteers, and they take the lead role in this part of the discussion. If this is done, it should be done at the meeting and not beforehand, to avoid the danger that others in the group fail to complete the prescribed reading.

8   Arrange the rota for handling the training sessions.

9   Close the meeting.

## Meeting 2

*Preparatory reading*

This book, Chapter 5   The basic requirements
         Chapter 6   Roles and resources
         Chapter 8   Section on 'group process'
                     (pages 119 to 128).

Members' handbook, Session 7   Working together

*The meeting*

1   Introduce whoever has been designated to take the training session 'Working together'. Explain to the group that the reason this session is being tackled at this stage is that it is particularly relevant to the role of facilitator and it will be as well to go through it now, so that the lessons it contains can be digested and used in forthcoming meetings.

2   Invite the relevant volunteer to take the group through the lesson on 'Working together'.

3   After the session, review the material, visual aids and lesson plan. Discuss the relevance of training in the skills of working together, to complement the problem-solving techniques themselves. Discuss when would be the appropriate time in the formation and training of a Circle to cover this topic.

4   Thank whoever ran the session.

5   Move the group on to a discussion of the role of the facilitator. Establish that everyone is quite clear about the role and the key requirement, which is to develop the Circle to independence. Discuss the likely problems from the point of view of both

facilitator behaviour (for example, building dependency) and the Circle itself.

6  Discuss and clarify the mechanics of the facilitator role, including the meetings which are required to do the job.

7  Introduce a discussion about group process, the understanding of which is the key to successful facilitation. Base the discussion on the reading on group process and try to encourage the group to think of actual examples from their experience, and, more importantly, from the present meeting.

8  Ask each member of the group to give one example of group process which has affected the present meeting. Go round the room and discuss the examples. Use this exercise, firstly, to ensure that everyone understands what group process involves, and, secondly, to start the process of talking about it. Introduce this part of the meeting by reinforcing the point that a big problem which leads to so many groups having problems is that we tend not to talk about what is really happening in the group, perhaps because the subject matter can be seen by some as being 'too hot to handle', or simply because many people have no understanding of the concept of group process. Whatever the reason, there is a need to legitimise critiquing and process observation in general. Developing our skills in this will benefit our work in any group we are associated with, including Quality Circles.

9  Establish a rule that any interesting or noteworthy example of group process from any future meetings should be highlighted, so that everyone can have the opportunity of developing his or her skills of process observation and feedback. Also establish the rule that each meeting will end with a critique.

10  Establish the preparatory reading for the next session

and close the meeting with a critique. Try to make sure that the critique is concerned with terms of process rather than task. It usually takes a few meetings for this to come about, and these periods can be used as learning periods to enhance understanding of process and its components.

## Meeting 3

*Preparatory reading*

This book, Chapter 7   The programme of introduction
Members' handbook, Session 2   Problem-solving
                                        Session 3   Brainstorming

*The meeting*

1   Introduce the concept of sound problem-solving structure as a prerequisite for a successful Quality Circle.
2   Have the appropriate participant take the rest of the group through the lesson on problem-solving.
3   Review the session in terms of material, visual aids and the recommended lesson plan.
4   Move on to the tape on 'Brainstorming'. Establish brainstorming as a core technique of Quality Circles and one it is vital for members of Quality Circles to understand and be proficient in. Go through the procedure again, including the review.
5   Go through the company's proposed plan of introduction, in detail, preferably using a prepared handout of the programme. Discuss the plan with the group, including estimated timings. Compare the plan with that outlined in Chapter 7 and establish the logic of the Company scheme.
6   Critique the meeting.

## Meeting 4

*Preparatory reading*

This book, Chapter 9   Training the leaders
Members' handbook, Session 4   Analysing problems
                            Session 5  Collecting data

*The meeting*

1   The lesson on 'Analysing problems' is probably the most complicated of the eight sessions. It is also vital, since it teaches the two techniques recommended for the detailed analysis of problems. It is especially important that facilitators feel comfortable with these two techniques, so that they, in their turn, can ensure that the lessons are soundly learned by leaders and members.

2   The appropriate person should take the group through the lesson on 'Analysing problems'.

3   The lesson should be reviewed in terms of content, visual aids and lesson planning. The technique likely to be of most use in different situations in the company, and the reasons why, should also be discussed at this point.

4   The emphasis should then switch to the next technique, 'Collecting data'. The importance of this lies in the need for data-based rather than opinion-based arguments.

5   The relevant volunteer should present the lesson on 'Collecting data'.

6   The lesson should be reviewed as before.

7   The next topic to be discussed is the proposed leader training course. The facilitators who ultimately take the first-stage Circles will attend the course, and it is important that there is a discussion before the event about the structure of the course and the role the facilitators will play in it. In some situations it is

sensible to have them join in with the volunteer leaders and act as normal course members. On other occasions it is better to keep the facilitators rather more on the sidelines of the course, practising their facilitative skills in the group work. Their roles should be discussed and decided during this meeting. One criterion for making this decision will be the number of potential leaders being trained. If it is low, the former option will be more appropriate, although undoubtedly there will be other factors to be taken into account as well.

8   Critique the meeting.

## Meeting 5

*Preparatory reading*

This book, Chapter 8   Section on 'planning meetings' (pages 128 to 131)

Chapter 8   Section on 'review meetings' (pages 131 to 139)

Members' handbook, Session 6   Presenting to management

*The meeting*

1   'Management presentations' are the logical culmination of the work of Quality Circles, and therefore need to be done well. Although initially the requirement is perceived by many Circle members, and even leaders, as quite threatening, it is surprising what a little experience can do for their confidence and competence, even to the extent that many derive great satisfaction and enjoyment from this aspect of Circle work.

2   The lesson should be presented and reviewed in terms of material, visual aids and lesson planning, in just the same way as previous sessions have been treated.

3   Having done this, the group should turn its attention to a key issue, that of the facilitator role in planning the Circle meetings with the leader. This topic should be debated against the background of the preparatory reading on the subject.
4   The next topic is equally vital and concerns the role of the facilitator in reviewing the Circle meetings afterwards. Again the discussion can be held against the background of the preparatory reading on the subject.
5   Critique the meeting.

**Meeting 6**

*Preparatory reading*

This book, Chapter 10   Management and Quality Circles
              Chapter 12   Problems and issues
Members' handbook, Session 8   Dealing with problems
                                in the Circle

*The meeting*

1   The last of the training tapes concentrates on what Circles should do if they find themselves in trouble. It is essential that facilitators, and leaders for that matter, have a good grasp of the recommended actions to take in the different problem circumstances, since it will obviously be better if the Circle can solve its difficulties for itself without recourse to the tape. The more informally problems can be dealt with the better.
2   The relevant person should go through the lesson, which should then be reviewed as usual.
3   A prime requirement for the success of a Circle programme in the medium and longer term is that management should 'buy in' to the concept and see it as an effective mechanism which helps to improve the performance of the department, amongst other things

by getting problems solved at the workplace and thus freeing management to deal with issues at its own level. One of the things many Circles find difficult at the beginning is making it easy for their managers to support them, and a key role of the facilitator is to ensure that this support is forthcoming. A discussion should take place on the basis of the preparatory reading, therefore, during which the potential problems should be reviewed and put into the current perspective. Preliminary plans, notably to ensure effective communication, can also be decided at this point.

4 Other problems which can affect the progress of the Quality Circles programme are detailed in Chapter 12, which should have been read. These should be reviewed and added to in the light of local knowledge, since to have those taking part in the programme aware of the possible dangers, and keeping a close watch for any early warning signs, will help to ensure that speedy action can be taken to deal with anything likely to damage the programme.

5 As this is the last of the formal induction and training sessions for facilitators, there is a need to decide who will actually facilitate the Circle being launched. Volunteers should, therefore, be sought. If there are too many, it should be the responsibility of the whole group, including the trainer, to come to a decision. A programme of communication meetings, so that everyone is kept up to date and informed, can also be arranged at this time, if a desire to do so is expressed, especially by those who will not be facilitating a group at this stage.

6 Critique the meeting.

## Group process

In all interactions within groups there are two main factors, the job to be done (the task) and something called group process, which is to do with how the group tackles the task. Most problems which occur in groups producing less than satisfactory performance are caused by problems of group process rather than any inability of members to cope with the task itself. Most people tend to be mesmerised by the task, whatever it is, and quite forget that it is the way the group works that is likely to have the greatest influence on its success.

The role of facilitator is very much concerned with ensuring that the Quality Circle does not forget group process in its drive to solve the problem being worked on. The training session on 'Working together' gives everyone the chance to get to grips with some of the principles of group process, or group dynamics, as it is sometimes known, and this section takes that learning a few stages further. A huge amount of research has been done on the subject of group working, however, and even a complete book on the subject could really only scratch the surface of what is a very complex area.

This section, therefore, concentrates on some of the variables which are likely to be having an effect on the Circle, and gives the facilitator the opportunity of identifying the key dynamics of the group and feeding them back. In this way the Circle can progressively take greater control of its own process, which is one sign of an effective group. Even in short group meetings there is so much process, so much is happening both at a conscious and unconscious level, that it would be impossible to analyse it all. Indeed, such an attempt would be fruitless, since there would be too much information for anyone to handle successfully. The facilitator, therefore, should concentrate on diagnosing the critical incidents in the group's work, the key dynamics, which had a substantial effect on how the group achieved, or failed to achieve, its task.

The job of isolating the key events, working out how and why they happened, and then of helping the group

120

to see the effect that they had, is not easy, not least because so often groups in the early stages of developing their awareness about group process tend not to see the same things happening as the outsider. Often it is as if the facilitator and the group have been in different meetings! It is here that great care is needed to avoid becoming trapped in a win/lose argument about what did and did not happen, about motives, cause and effect and a whole plethora of rationalisations which cannot serve to move the group forward. The task of the facilitator is not only to observe and diagnose effectively, it is also to have the necessary sensitivity and skill to aid the learning of the relevant lessons, to make it easy for Circle leaders and members to become more proficient at controlling the dynamics of their meetings, and thereby to help the group towards secure self-sufficiency.

Probably the best way to diagnose the process of a group is to have some sort of mental checklist containing the likely key dimensions of the type of group being considered. Although group dynamics concern the whole group, some of the ingredients have more to do with individual behaviour, and so it is convenient to look at group process in the light, firstly, of the effect of individual behaviour on it, and, secondly, of factors which are more to do with the group in its entirety or sub-sections of it.

Firstly, then, let us consider the important influences that individuals can have on group process. These can best be viewed under four main headings, as follows.

### *Activity level*
In any group there will be those that are more actively involved than others; some talk a lot, others are quieter. Often the balance changes during a meeting, and there is always a reason for this. In many groups it seems to be up to one or two individuals to keep the group moving forward, and it is important to know why this is so and

121

what effect it is having on the group. There is nothing intrinsically wrong with there being high and low participators in a group, as long as no one is being excluded and as long as there are members of the group fulfilling the so-called 'gatekeeping' role and helping people to get into the discussion if they want to. A problem which sometimes occurs in groups, however, is that some people fulfil a 'gateclosing' role, shutting group members out. Where this happens, and it can happen subtly, it is obviously vital to diagnose and correct it quickly.

The key questions about individual levels of participation are, therefore:

1   Are the more active participants hogging the discussion?
2   Is anyone who could make a useful contribution being excluded?
3   Is enough work being done to encourage quieter members to contribute? Often they are the ones who have the greatest insight, because they have listened to all the contributions to date.

### *Kinds of influence*

Level of participation is not the same as influence. Quite often people who talk a lot are not really listened to, and have very little influence over other group members, and vice versa. This is an important part of process, as is the method of influencing the group. Some people try to force their own opinions on others regardless of their views, which is called self-authorised behaviour. Other people prefer a democratic style and want to ensure that everyone has a say. Some individuals try to influence the group by refusing to be drawn in, and this kind of negative influence can obviously have a serious effect on the group as a whole.

The key questions here, then, are:

1   Who are the influential group members?

2   Why is this? Is it because of their knowledge of the subject or for other reasons? What are the other reasons?
3   What styles of influence are used in the group? Which are accepted and which are rejected by other members?
4   Do the styles of influence of dominant members fit in with the desire and expectation of the rest of the group, or is a win/lose relationship developing between different people on the basis of the method being used to try to influence the rest?

## Defensiveness

We all use defence mechanisms to avoid having to come to terms with what is really happening. Sometimes they are used consciously, but often they operate at an unconscious level. The latter are difficult to treat, since there is a likelihood that any feedback of a direct kind will be rejected. Nonetheless, they have a serious effect on the work of groups and need to be understood.

Defence mechanisms apply to individuals and to groups. As far as individuals are concerned the most common are the following:

1   *Rationalisation.* Someone substitutes a phoney reason for the real one, to avoid either consciously or unconsciously having to cope with the implications of the real reason. An example could be, 'The reason the presentation went badly was that the projector bulb broke', rather than, 'We didn't have a spare bulb and we didn't perform very well'. Another example could be, 'The reason my group performed badly was that my members were not up to the task', rather than, 'I did not lead, train and motivate them well enough'.
2   *Withdrawal.* A physical symptom of this mechanism often occurs when someone moves his chair back, or sits back in his chair. Some people leave groups

123

because they feel they cannot handle what is happening; and where this happens, it is also a defence mechanism. Obviously there are other reasons for leaving a group as well, so it is not possible to say that anyone who leaves is behaving defensively. Other symptoms of withdrawal are boredom and refusal to enter into the work of the group.

3 *Cynicism.* Usually made manifest by questioning whether the work being done is worthwhile. Someone who says, 'It's not worth it, they'll just say no at the end of the day' could be really saying, 'I'm not sure I can handle this way of working'.

4 *Generalisation.* The tendency to make generalised statements about what is happening, or what has happened, rather than being specific. Someone who was very worried about playing his part in a management presentation could say, 'I'm not sure presentations should be a part of Circle work because people can get quite worried about them'.

5 *Competition.* Competition within the group is a relatively common phenomenon, as is competing with the leader or facilitator. Inappropriate competition has its roots in win/lose and often is a way of someone saying to himself, 'No one could blame me for what is happening; it's all their fault!'

As has been said, we are all defensive. No one should be allowed to feel flawed or demeaned by the assumption that we all need defence mechanisms. There are times, however, when they are counter-productive and need dealing with. In diagnosing counter-productive defensiveness the facilitator will need to put the behaviour he sees into the wider context of the meeting, and the possible threats that any group member might feel. The key questions here include:

(1) Is this really what the member of the group wanted to say or do?

(2) If defensiveness is indicated, is it detrimental to the progress being made by the group? If not, leave it alone.

### Getting the job done

Within any group someone must ensure that things get done and that the group remains on target. There is no point in having a very happy group that has enjoyable meetings and yet achieves nothing. There are a number of different requirements here, from making sure that the problem-solving structure is appropriate, to keeping the group on target and concentrating on the task at hand. Often there will be more than one person in the group who fulfils roles like these, and this is fine as long as no role conflict is generated.

Key questions regarding this problem include:

1  Is anyone keeping the facts and the discussion updated and in front of the group by summarising the situation to date?
2  Is anyone ensuring that all the relevant data, whether they be facts, opinions or alternative solutions, are being collected?
3  Is someone making sure that the problem-solving structure being used is suitable for the task?
4  Do members keep hopping from one subject to another, thus stopping the group from making progress down its chosen path?

Some aspects of group dynamics, of course, are affected by the whole group or sub-groups rather than individuals, and it is to the most important of these that we shall now turn.

### Atmosphere

That groups have an atmosphere would be readily accepted by most people who have ever been in one. Equally there would be widespread agreement that the kind of atmosphere can have an important effect on the group concerned. It is vital, therefore, for the facilitator to get a sense of the atmosphere and what is affecting it. Some groups get into the habit of having congenial meetings, where everyone gets on well and yet nothing gets done. Others are cold and clinical, and not necessarily any more effective. The atmosphere in a group will spring from many causes, and the questions to ask include:

1  What effect are the physical surroundings having?
2  What effect is the task the group is engaged in having?
3  To what extent do members feel able to make contributions without fear of being made to look foolish or being ignored?
4  What is the leader's contribution to the atmosphere in the group?
5  How much of the business of the group seems to be done above the table and how much under it?

### Sub-grouping
A potentially dangerous possibility for the morale and effectiveness of the group is sub-grouping. This can occur for a number of reasons, and almost invariably leads to the formation of 'in groups' and 'out groups', which can so easily lead the group itself into an unproductive and debilitating win/lose situation. Sub-grouping is relatively easy to diagnose although the underlying motivations of the participants may not be clear. It is important not to overreact where sub-groups are formed, especially if they are 'one off' events. It is when they start to become habitual, with the same 'in groups' and 'out groups', that the situation needs to be dealt with.

Key questions to ask in diagnosing serious sub-grouping include:

1  Is there any consistent agreement or disagreement between sub-groups?

2   Is there an élite within the group? If so, how does it treat the rest of the group?

3   Is there a sub-group which is vying for leadership of the group? If so, is there one individual behind it?

4   Do the same sub-groups always form over the same issues: for example, the choice of problem to be tackled next, finger-pointing at other departments, or organising roles for the management presentations?

5   Are the sub-groups helping or hindering the group as a whole? Is the whole group in control of this aspect of its process, and can it cope with the implications?

6   Is there any straightforward 'ganging up'? If so, urgent action is needed.

### Group rules

Any group which meets on a regular basis develops rules that members abide by. These rules, or norms as they are usually called, are often unspoken, and yet they are inviolable for anyone who wishes to continue as a member. Sometimes a norm will only be recognised by some of the members, and occasionally it can happen that no one is really aware of some of the prevailing 'rules'. An 'open' norm that many Circles choose to make explicit is 'no criticism'. Clearly it is necessary for the facilitator to have a good idea of what the important norms are, firstly, so that he does not violate them himself, and, secondly, so that he can better understand the behaviour of the group.

Important diagnostic questions here include:

1   What are the explicit rules that members agree to abide by?

2   What sanctions does the group impose on members who transgress? Are the sanctions counter-productive?

3   What seem to be the unspoken rules? Would it help the group to make them explicit? Sometimes the

127

answer to this question is a definite 'no'. We should not automatically think that openness is a good thing.

4  Are there any subjects that seem to be taboo? Does this materially affect the work of the group?

5  Do any of the unspoken norms seem to contravene any of the core principles of Quality Circles?

6  Are there any norms to do with the expression of the feelings of group members? Being able to express feelings is an important part of being an effective group. If this is taboo, something will probably need to be done.

This section is not intended to be a comprehensive treatment of group process. That would take an encyclopedia. What it attempts to do is to highlight aspects of the subject which are likely to have practical value to the facilitator of Quality Circles. The topics covered in the training session on 'Working together' have not been repeated, so this is additional material.

There are many books and articles on group working and group process. It is a subject which has a fascination all of its own, one where it is almost impossible to lay down hard and fast rules and yet where there are so many generalisations that always seem to come true. It is also a subject, fortunately or unfortunately, where the more one learns, the more one realises how little one knows. For the Quality Circle facilitator to be successful, a working knowledge of group process is required. This section, allied to the training session on 'Working together', will provide a foundation to build on.

## Planning meetings

The role of preparation is vital in making presentations to management. It is equally important with normal Circle meetings. To go into a meeting of the group unprepared will undoubtedly have a negative effect on the progress made by the group, and is likely to make for a unsatisfactory meeting. In the early days one of the roles of the facilitator is to assist the leader in the planning of the meetings, and to develop the latter's skill in this area, so that preparedness becomes a matter of course before Circle, or any other, meetings.

As might be expected, the time taken in preparation for meetings decreases as experience and skill are developed. At the start, up to an hour should be set aside. After three or four months the figure is often as low as fifteen minutes. It is vital that sufficient time is set aside, in the early days especially, when the meetings often contain a high element of training as well as other business. If the training is not done well, the group will not have the tools to do the job; lack of tools may very well reduce the performance of the Circle, and perhaps lead to its demise. To risk a Circle, indeed a whole programme, for the sake of the amount of time and care needed at the beginning is to 'spoil the ship for a ha'porth of tar'.

The preparation meetings between facilitator and leader should be run by the leader to a degree commensurate with the development of his skills. In many cases the facilitator will need to make the running at the beginning. The first step in preparing the meeting is to set it in context. Examination of which stage of the problem-solving cycle has been reached is an important consideration here, as well as the extent of the development of the group as a group. The ability to look further ahead than the next meeting is the ability alluded to, and it is important if the Circle is to fulfil its full potential. The next step is to come to a view about what needs to be done at the next meeting, followed by the detailed preparation of who will do and say what. In the early stages the Circle members will probably need training in one or other of the techniques, and since this is such an important activity, we shall take this situation as our model.

Let us assume, then, that training in one or other of the

techniques is required. The next stage should be to read the teaching background in the relevant session of the training manual, which will put the subject into context and give hints as to the handling of the meeting and the recommended timings. The following stage should be to review the tape itself. Ideally this should be done by playing it through and showing the visual aids. The leader is the best person to handle the changing of the visual aids, since doing so will reinforce his position as leader of the group, and, in the early stages, this is important, to give the group a focus and also to help the development of the leader's confidence in the role. It is advisable for him to practise the physical movements and timing of changing the slides or overhead transparencies, since some dexterity is required, and one does not want problems arising during the meeting itself. An alternative to playing the tape through, although it is a second best option, is to read the relevant lesson plan in the training manual to remind oneself of the structure and content of the lesson.

Having done this, the leader and facilitator should agree on how to handle the meeting. Firstly, the meeting plan needs to be drawn up, with rough timings for the various parts of the meeting. Once the meeting plan has been settled, decisions are required as to the roles to be adopted during the meeting. At all times the rule of thumb here should be that the leader handles as much as he or she feels capable of, since the ability to run the meetings is an essential step towards self-sufficiency, and needs to be developed as quickly as is reasonably possible, given the personality, skill and previous experience of the leader in question. Although the requirement will vary from person to person, it is very strongly recommended that at least the bones of the lesson plan are written and taken into the meeting. Notes on the structure of the meeting can help to improve the flow of events as well as being a useful 'crutch' in the event of the leader suffering a mental block, something which can happen to anyone, however experienced. Some people feel comfortable with fuller notes, some will be happy with a skeleton – the important thing is to have something. One method is to take a photocopy of the lesson plan from the relevant section of the training manual and to add the specific notes relating to the Circle in question.

Since all the leaders and facilitators will, by the time they come to run a session, have been through all the training tapes, they will be well aware, from the session on 'Working together', that another important aspect of the preparation for any meeting concerns the physical amenities and layout of the room. After a few meetings it should become second nature to check the room, seating, availability of projector if needed, flip chart, pens and so on.

Finally, it is worth spending a few moments considering an issue which occasionally arises: people may ask how it is possible to plan ahead when it is up to Circle members to decide how best they should spend their time. The answer is that Circle members, of whom the leader is one, still control the group and can influence the way the group works and what it works on. The preparation for the meetings is designed to lay out the framework which is most likely to assist the group in its work and help it to move forward; in no way should it attempt to manipulate the group into a previously determined decision or course of action.

There is sometimes a temptation to skimp on the preparation for meetings. Do not let this happen as far as the Circles are concerned. Circles are organised, disciplined, problem-solving groups; preparation is vital for their success.

## Review meetings
The review meeting, which should take place as soon

131

after the Circle meeting as possible, represents the culmination of the work of the facilitator. During this meeting the lessons which lead to the development of the Circle leader are learned. It is often a difficult meeting to handle if done well, but it is invariably easy if treated at a simplistic level, since only the 'skin surface' issues will be brought out. There are two main potential problems related to the meeting: one is isolating the key dynamics of the Circle meeting in the first place, and the second is the process of feeding them back. This section will focus on the latter, since it will be assumed that the section on group process will have assisted the accurate diagnosis of the Circle meeting itself.

The purpose of feeding back data is to help the recipient to improve his performance next time round. It is a process of influence, therefore, and the method used to initiate this process will materially affect the outcome. A useful method, which can help the facilitator think-through his style of influence, proposes that the response of the person being influenced can be to comply with the attempt at influence, to respond positively out of identification with the influencer, or to internalise the proposed action, and that it will be the style of influence which is a main determinant of the outcome. The importance of which outcome occurs lies in the fact that the commitment of the person being influenced is radically affected by the different responses.

The highest quality of response, and the one which will generate the highest commitment to action, is internalisation. In effect, this means that the person concerned alters his behaviour because he wants to. He perceives the change as being his own. To respond out of identification is to do something out of admiration or respect for the influencer. To comply is to do something because one has been told to or one percieves that one should, whether or not one wants to. The likely level o' commitment of these two latter responses will be significantly lower. The problem with identification is that it tends to last only while the influencer is present, but this reaction is probably preferable to compliance, where the level of commitment will always be low and the new behaviour is likely to be quickly forgotten as soon as the pressure to change is removed. With this in mind, the facilitator should, wherever possible, be aiming for an internalised response from the Circle leader, and this is where the difficulty often lies, since to achieve this requires the utmost facilitative skill. To put it bluntly, anyone, given the power, can tell someone what to do; it is quite another matter to help that person to his own conclusions.

The main difficulty of facilitation is that the natural style of most people is the 'tell and sell' one that is most likely to lead to compliance or even outright rejection. The style of facilitation, to be really successful, usually needs to be more delicate than telling the Circle leader what he did wrong and what he has to do to put it right. The problem with this style is not necessarily that either the diagnosis or the solution is wrong, it is simply one of ownership. If all the mental activity which has gone into identifying the problem and finding the cure has gone on in the head of the facilitator, it should hardly be surprising if the ownership lies with him rather than the Circle leader. An alternative style for the facilitator is to invite the leader to assess his own performance and to make his own plans for improvement wherever possible. Thus the mental activity to diagnose the performance of the leader goes on in the leader's head, while the facilitator is working hard to help him think it through.

If the leader diagnoses his own performance and makes his own plans for improvement, his commitment is likely to be very high. If the facilitator raises an issue and the leader solves it, there will be commitment, although not at the same level. If the facilitator raises the issues and solves them, the commitment of the leader is not likely to be very great. The facilitator should remember this sequence when he is reviewing Circle meetings with the leader. A typical example of what can happen if this lesson is not learned is given below.

*Facilitator*: Did you find the meeting easy to handle?
*Leader*:  Yes, I did for most of the time, especially when the group was working on the design of the check sheet. It got a bit sticky at the end when they were all firing questions at me.
*Facilitator*: Yes, well, I thought they were a rabble, all cross-talking and having little sub-group meetings. They've got to learn, or else there really is no point.
*Leader*:  Well, you have to remember that they are all men; it's different with the other Circles here, they have women in them and women react differently.
*Facilitator*: That's not the point. What you have to do is to confront them with their behaviour, and tell them that they had better sort themselves out.
*Leader*:  Yes, but they are a strong-minded group and men react differently from women. You can't judge this group by comparing it to other Circles in the Company. How do you rate this group against the other Circles?
*Facilitator*: That's irrelevant, it's this group I'm concerned about.

At this point the outside consultant intervened.

It was clear that there *was* a lot of cross-talking in this group, and the meeting was, in some parts, ill-disciplined. The feedback of the facilitator, however, did little that would have led to any committed behaviour change. Hindsight, of course, is 20/20, but it is perhaps worth looking at an alternative way of tackling this kind of feedback.

*Facilitator*: How did you see the meeting?

| | |
|---|---|
| *Leader*: | I found it quite easy for most of the time, especially when the group was working on the design of the check sheet. It got a bit sticky at the end when they were all firing questions at me. |
| *Facilitator*: | What were your feelings when that was happening? |
| *Leader*: | Well, I felt pressurised with everyone talking at once, and, well, out of control of the meeting, I suppose. |
| *Facilitator*: | What was the real problem you were feeling then? |
| *Leader*: | It was everyone talking at once, I suppose. It's very difficult out there at the front to think as well as talk and the whole thing was very confusing. |
| *Facilitator*: | Groups really are very complicated things and it takes a lot of time to develop our skills at working with them. What possibilities might there be for solving the problem of everyone talking at once? |
| *Leader*: | I don't know, you're the expert, why don't you tell me? |
| *Facilitator*: | Well, I'm not sure that I am the expert, but anyway I think that what might be the right thing for one person to do as leader of a group might well be entirely wrong for someone else. These things are usually a matter of individual style. |
| *Leader*: | I suppose I could just say, 'Can we have one person talking at a time?' but I don't want to cut anyone off; after all it is their group as well as mine. |
| *Facilitator*: | It is very difficult, I agree. The leader of a Circle has a very complex role, being both a member of the group, and the leader as well, with all that that entails. One of the.... |
| *Leader*: | Of course, one of the jobs of a leader should |

135

|  | |
|---|---|
| | be to keep order and make sure the meeting goes OK, so I could do it. |
| *Facilitator:* | And make sure everyone gets a chance to speak. |
| *Leader:* | I could do with being a summariser as well, so that we stay on track. Yes, that's quite helpful; yet it seems too simple. Will it work? |
| *Facilitator:* | Is there any reason why it shouldn't? |
| *Leader:* | I expected it to be more complicated than that, though; do you know what I mean? |
| *Facilitator:* | Sure do. Maybe it would be as well to jot down the things we've agreed so that we can review them over the next few weeks and see how they work. |
| *Leader:* | Makes sense. |

In this example, the facilitator has tried to get the leader to diagnose and solve his own problem, and has taken a supportive stance while this has been going on. The leader is not being manipulated into predetermined answers, the facilitator is trying to help him find his own solutions and is backing these up by building on them. The comment about making sure everyone gets a chance to speak is an instance. For the purpose of this feedback meeting the Circle leader is the 'centre of the universe' as far as the facilitator is concerned, and that is just as it should be. A facilitator is a resource and a helper. He is not there to get his own way, to satisfy his status needs by appearing to be clever, or to be 'the expert'. If he can genuinely make the group and the leader the centre of his universe for the requisite period of time, he will learn much about people, himself and the process of facilitation.

Review meetings are a key part of the development of self-sufficient Quality Circles. They represent the main chance the facilitator has of encouraging the growth of the leader's skills, based on actual experience.

Whereas it is preferable for the facilitator to use his skill to help the Circle leader think through the possibilities for improvement and to develop his own action plans, there will be occasions when this strategy will be inappropriate. The role of facilitator will ultimately be judged in terms of success in the development of a self-sufficient group, and as such it must be flexible. Sometimes the strategy of encouraging the leader to diagnose the potential for improvement, and then to provide the action plan, will be found wanting. Supervisors who are new to the role or who are particularly lacking in confidence might have to be dealt with by alternative methods. Whatever other way of dealing with the problem is chosen, however, its objective should be to develop the particular leader to the stage where he is able to diagnose and solve his own problems. There is no point in solving people's problems for them if the ultimate objective is to develop them to self-sufficiency.

Where it becomes apparent that the leader is not yet in a position to diagnose and solve his own difficulties, there will probably be a natural tendency to return to the 'tell and sell' model. Such a move should be resisted, however, for it is quite possible that the leader is capable of either diagnosing the problem, or providing the solution once he has been given the diagnosis. If this does prove to be the case, the outcome is likely to be better than that which could be expected from 'tell and sell'. Furthermore, this level of ownership by the leader is more 'advanced' than that usually forthcoming with 'tell and sell', and so it should be that much more possible to develop the leader on to full-scale diagnosis and solution of his own difficulties.

One of the many important keys to success in the facilitator role is likely to be the talking ratio – the proportion of time during the discussion that he spends talking as opposed to listening. With the 'tell and sell' method there is a tendency for the facilitator to do most of the talking, since it is he that is producing the ideas. In consequence, there is a lower level of commitment in the leader. Studies have shown that where the facilitator does less than 40 per cent of the talking, a number of important outcomes may result:

1   There is a greater likelihood of constructive action, notably when the leader is fully engaged in setting his own targets.
2   There will not be many arguments.
3   The leader will feel more motivated.
4   Both facilitator and leader will feel more positive about each other.
5   It is more likely that the leader will be able to diagnose his own problems.
6   The facilitator will learn more about the leader and this knowledge will lead to his assessing the leader's performance more favourably.

Facilitator performance in review meetings is difficult to assess unless someone else attends an occasional meeting. It is notoriously difficult, for example, to estimate how much time one has spent talking in a meeting, as opposed to listening, and many people quite genuinely get it the wrong way round – in other words they spend 70 per cent of the time talking and claim to have listened for that proportion of the time. Since the skills associated with facilitation are of great value to any manager, as well as being important to the success of Quality Circles, it is likely that the facilitators will welcome any opportunity to develop their skills to a higher level. Where outside consultants are used in the programme, they should be present at occasional review meetings, but even when the programme is resourced entirely from within, there is a strong case for either the trainer, co-ordinator or indeed another facilitator to sit in occasionally at both the Circle and the review meeting, to give the facilitator the opportunity of a sounding board to voice his own thoughts and also the benefit of any feedback from his colleagues. The leader can often also be a fertile ground for feedback, though, of course, it must remain clear that the fundamental purpose of the meeting is to develop the leader, and consequently the Circle, to independence.

The focus of this section has been, quite deliberately, on the process aspects of the review meeting. Clearly, however, there is a need to discuss task aspects and to ensure that the Circle is making sufficient progress at solving its chosen problems, since it is this aspect which will directly affect member motivation.

One task aspect of special importance is the choice of problem itself. For the first few rounds of problem-solving it is likely that there will be a fairly obvious contender, and that the group will find it relatively easy to choose. A vital part of the long-term development of the Circle, however, will be the extent to which the group begins to see its role in the light of a general effort to make things better, even if they are reasonably satisfactory already. The Circle whose members believe that they can trim 10 per cent off the already reasonable scrap rate, and which adopts this as a project, is really beginning to put itself in an entirely positive win/win role. For most groups, however, this will not happen automatically, and there is likely to be a tendency to stick with sorting out problems rather than exploiting opportunities. A key role of the facilitator, therefore, is progressively to encourage leader and members alike to widen their horizons and to take on the fuller challenge offered, and this matter should be broached at the review meeting periodically, notably when the Circle is beginning to need a new problem to work on.

# Chapter 9

# TRAINING THE LEADERS

There is, quite obviously, no readily available method which will develop effective Circle leaders immediately; what is needed is a process of training and development, which will enable individuals to learn and practise new skills at their own pace. The training of Quality Circle leaders usually takes place over a period of five or six months, and is a major role of the facilitator. At the outset, however, potential leaders will need to be trained in, one, the problem-solving structure and techniques, and, two, the skills associated with developing and running an effective group. The training is best accomplished within the framework of a normal training course, which should be attended by both potential leaders and facilitators. It has already been stated that more supervisors should be trained than Circles it is intended to start, which has the added advantage of making for a better training event, since the ideal number attending a course is between eight and fifteen.

It is often worth engaging outside consultants to run the training course. If the company believes it has the internal capacity, however, the programme would probably be run by the training manager or the co-ordinator of the progamme.

There should be five main objectives of the course. The first is to induct potential leaders into the problem-solving techniques of Quality Circles. The second is to give them practice in using the techniques and thus to boost their confidence and competence. The third objective is to give some instruction in group process. The fourth is to get the facilitators engaged in Circle work with the potential leaders. The fifth is to find volunteers to start up Circles at the end of the course, and to decide who will do so.

The remainder of this chapter deals in detail with the recommended two and a half day training event, which can be held either in plant or away from it. The contents could be squeezed into two days if two evenings were included, but this would probably make the course too intensive for many participants.

## Course administration

It is important that any course runs smoothly, for there is nothing more frustrating for trainers or trainees than muddles that could have been avoided.

A decision is required at the outset on whether the master copies of the visual aids, contained in the training package, should be made into overhead projector transparencies, 35 mm slides or flip charts. Clearly the same technology should be used for training both the leaders and Circle members. Once the decision has been made, the slides, overhead transparencies or flip charts need to be produced and checked for quality.

The following list of requirements for the course is basic, and may be added to if necessary:

1 Arrangements for a senior manager to open the course.
2 Arrangements for one or two senior managers to attend the management presentations on the last day of the course.
3 One room large enough to hold the number attending in comfort, arranged in a horseshoe facing the trainer's materials.
4 One or two syndicate rooms located near the main

room. Whether one or two are required will depend on the size of the course. As a rule of thumb, get two additional rooms if there are more than twelve coming on the course.

5 An overhead projector, slide projector or stand for the flip charts, depending on how the visual aids are presented, for the main room and each syndicate room.
6 A tape recorder for each room used.
7 A flip chart for each room used.
8 Masking tape.
9 Spare projector bulbs.
10 Scribbling pads and pencils for participants.
11 The training package from the QC programme. This contains all the teaching material for the eight problem-solving techniques, including audio tapes, recommended lesson plans and master copies of the visual aids.
12 A copy of the members' handbook for each participant. This book will act as the basic handout for people attending the course.
13 Photocopies of the training material as required.
14 Other handouts as required.

Good course administration is a prerequisite for success in launching a Quality Circle programme, and skimping on it can be disastrous.

## Course content

In this section we shall consider each session of the recommended leader course in detail, including lesson plans and any additional handouts which may be required for participants. The course as laid out is designed to run for two and a half days. Meals and refreshment breaks should be fitted in as required. The programme offers a sound induction to the role of Quality Circle leader. It can be added to as appropriate, depending on

the previous training which has been given to the people
in question, although care should be taken to ensure that
the training does not stray from the highly practical. If it
does, there may be problems in translating the apparently
easy theory into practice in the substantial complexities of
the real world. The course, as laid out, is very practical, it
deals with what Quality Circle leaders 'will' be doing in
their future activities, not what they 'should' achieve, or
'might' try.

### Session 1 – Introduction – fifteen minutes

*Background*
At the beginning of the course it is essential to demonstrate to those attending that Quality Circles are felt to be
important by senior people in the company. The senior
person on site, therefore, should make himself available
to open the course. It is also sensible in large companies
where people do not necessarily know each other to
make a short time available for general introductions.

*Lesson plan*
1  The trainer should convene the course and introduce
   the senior manager, who should then start the
   programme with a few words to indicate his or her
   commitment to the concept and view of what Quality
   Circles can achieve for the company. He or she can
   then leave the room.
2  If needed, everyone on the course should spend a
   minute or so jotting down a few notes about
   themselves, by way of introduction, and then
   introduce themselves to everyone. This is often worth
   doing, even if the participants do know each other, to
   break the ice, and get everyone speaking at least a few
   words. The important things to mention in the
   introduction include the area worked in, the perception the supervisor holds of his or her job, and the
   number of people working in the section. The trainer

143

should also take a turn in introducing himself to everyone. The distinction should be made between facilitators and potential leaders.

3  The trainer should explain that the course is going to be participative and that anyone who has a comment, observation or question should bring it up at the time, so that the whole event is a discussion rather than a series of lectures.

### Session 2 – Course objectives – fifteen minutes

*Background*
On many courses the objectives are not made clear, and this omission can seriously affect understanding. A pre-prepared visual aid should be used. The course handout (the members' handbook) should be given out at the beginning, so that people can get used to using it.

*Lesson plan*
1  It should be stated that to have clear objectives from the start will assist everyone's learning, and also help a useful evaluation of the course to be carried out at the end, to see to what extent the goals have been achieved.

2  The visual aid should be displayed, clarified and discussed as needed. Any additional objectives suggested by course members should be considered and added, if appropriate. The main objectives should be:

(a) To induct the potential leaders in the problem-solving techniques.
(b) To give the opportunity of using the techniques.
(c) To introduce participants to the key elements of group dynamics.
(d) To get the potential facilitators and leaders working together on Quality Circles.
(e) To encourage the potential leaders to want to start a Quality Circle.

Subsidiary objectives related to the facilitators can be added if required.

3   The members' handbook should be introduced, and a copy handed out to everyone. The structure of the book and its role for both leaders and Circle members should be discussed.

### Session 3 – Teaching adults – thirty minutes

*Background*
From the outset it should be made clear that one of the key reasons for going through the problem-solving techniques is to be able to teach them to Circle members. If they are not taught successfully, the Circles will not have the tools to do the job of solving problems in an organised way. Furthermore, it needs to be recognised that teaching adults is not the same as teaching children.

*Lesson plan*
1   Introduce the idea that there are two reasons for going through the problem-solving techniques. One is to learn them ourselves, and the second is to consider the best way of teaching them to Circle members. Introduce the idea that wherever possible it should be the job of the Circle leader to take the lead in training Circle members. Explain that this is not nearly as frightening a prospect as it might appear, since there is ample back-up material available in the shape of audio tapes, visual aids and recommended lesson plans.
2   Introduce and discuss the different types of teaching method. These include learning 'parrot fashion', and learning by listening, seeing, doing or experiencing. Discuss the merits of the main ones in terms of teaching Quality Circle members. Experience shows that immediate reinforcement of lessons learned, through using the technique in a real situation, is vital to successful learning in most cases.

3   Explore the likely need for repetition and revision of training lessons, both for ourselves and Circle members. Make sure that the need to do this is not seen as a sign of stupidity or weakness. It is absolutely normal, and is the reason for backing up all training with course handouts. The handout in this case is the members' handbook.

### Session 4 – Introduction to the training material – five minutes

*Background*
Potential leaders may be rather overawed by the prospect of training Circle members, and it is very important that this requirement is made as unthreatening as possible.

*Lesson plan*
1   The training package should be displayed, and each item introduced in turn:

   (a) the audio tapes;
   (b) the visual aids;
   (c) the background and introduction to the techniques (in the training manual);
   (d) the recommended lesson plans (in the training manual);
   (e) the transcripts (in the training manual and the members' handbook).

2   Explain that the material will be freely available to Circle leaders to prepare and run the training sessions in Circle meetings.
3   Explain that the material is not the only help available. A facilitator will be assigned to each Circle to work with the leader for as long as it takes to make the Circle an effective and independent group. He will also help with the training if required.
4   State that everyone will have the chance to use the material during the two days of the course.

## Session 5 – An introduction to Quality Circles – forty-five minutes

*Background*
Although everyone will have attended the introductory talk on Quality Circles, it is likely that they will have forgotten some of the details of the approach. It is vital therefore to run through the introduction and revise the principles involved. Since this will be a key session to run, in terms of getting volunteers, it will be advisable to discuss how to handle it in practice.

*Lesson plan*
1   The materials required to run the first training session using the audio tape should be collected together and organised, so that the group can see how simple the task is.
2   It should be explained that it is intended to run through the tape exactly as recommended in the lesson plan, and that the group will discuss its effectiveness afterwards.
3   Run the tape as recommended in the lesson plan in Session 1 of the training manual, including the optional stop.
4   After the tape has finished, ask for views about the tape, the visual aids and the general construction of the lesson. Emphasise that the tapes, visual aids and lesson plans are resources to be used as required in the particular situation. Adapting them for use is perfectly in order.

## Session 6 – Preparation – ninety minutes

*Background*
This session gives everyone the experience of using the training material. The trainer and facilitator should ensure during the preparations that no one feels threatened or overawed.

*Lesson plan*

1  Explain that one of the advantages of holding a course such as this is that it gives everyone the opportunity of practising the techniques and different teaching methods in an environment where it does not matter if we make a few mistakes.

2  Introduce the idea that everyone should have the chance of preparing and running at least part of a session to train the rest of the group in one of the techniques. Explain that three of the sessions will be handled in this way. Divide the potential leaders up into three syndicates and allocate one of the following sessions to each:

(a) problem-solving;
(b) data collection;
(c) presenting to management.

Ask each group to prepare a session lasting forty-five minutes to train the other members of the group in the particular topic. Where the training material calls for the group to apply the technique to the problem in hand, the syndicates should be encouraged to invent suitable examples to work on. State that the facilitators will be available to help as needed.

3  Recommend that the best way to handle the task is as follows:

(a) Play the tape through, following it in the members' handbook to get a broad understanding of the subject and the visual aids.
(b) Review the contents within the syndicate.
(c) Read through the teaching background to the subject and consider the points at which it is recommended that the tape be stopped.
(d) Develop a lesson plan which has everyone in the syndicate taking part at some stage. It is usually

best to hand over at the break points, although this is not strictly necessary.

(e) Prepare relevant sections individually.
(f) Have a run through.
(g) Write up a 'headline' version of the programme on the flip chart.

4 State that there are almost ninety minutes available for the preparation of the lessons. Allocate the groups to different syndicate rooms and explain that there is a tape recorder, equipment for visual aids, and other materials available for each group.

Hand out the relevant visual aids for the subject in question, together with photocopies of the relevant chapter of the training manual.

5 During the preparatory phase the facilitators should be allocated to groups to help the process. The trainer should usually have a 'roving brief' to ensure that everyone is getting on all right. Facilitators should be reminded that it is not their role to take over and lead the meeting. They should, however, be prepared to give assistance and advice as requested and required. The trainer should try to make sure that any examples chosen by the syndicates for the whole group to work on are suitable.

### Session 7 – Problem-solving – sixty minutes

*Background*
This training module lays out the recommended problem-solving structures for Quality Circles to use. It focuses on two main areas. The first is the need to be in an appropriate frame of mind (for example, to avoid making assumptions about what others are thinking, to get out of the habit of blaming other people by pointing fingers at them, to concentrate on solving our own problems, the things we can influence, and, finally, to work towards a

situation where it is possible for everyone to win, and, therefore, to reduce unproductive 'them and us' behaviour).

The second aspect of problem-solving covered is the problem-solving structure itself – a ten-step procedure beginning with brainstorming the list of problems and ending with monitoring the results of the solution after it has been introduced. It is a complete sequence to ensure that problems are not only identified but analysed in an organised way, and that solutions are devised and sold to management. Then, if management agrees, the solution is implemented and the results monitored.

This is one of the sessions that will be taught by a syndicate. There is a need to ensure that they feel comfortable and that they receive positive feedback about their performance.

*Lesson plan*
1   Introduce this session as one being tackled by a syndicate, and ask the members to come up and set the room out as they need it. Then ask them to deliver the lesson.
2   During the session make notes of specific points that were handled particularly well, and of anything that did not come over clearly.
3   After the lesson has been completed, congratulate the syndicate on its performance, and say that a further ten or fifteen minutes will be spent on discussing any matters arising from the content of the material or the treatment of the material by the syndicate.
4   Ask for any general comments from the rest of the group regarding the way the lesson was handled. Give examples of points that were handled well.
5   Spend a little time revising the material itself, discussing such questions as whether the structure outlined makes sense and whether it is handled adequately in the tape and the visual aids.

## Session 8 – Brainstorming – sixty minutes

*Background*
Brainstorming is one of the core techniques associated with Quality Circles, and it is important, therefore, that people get it firmly 'under their belts'. It is best that the trainer runs this session, because of its importance and also because it is a very full session, and requires careful control of time.

Brainstorming, although used extensively by Quality Circles, was invented in the 1930s by Alex Osborn as a way of encouraging creative thought in small problem-solving groups. The technique is widely known but is often not used effectively. The module in the training package is suitable for use in other contexts but, for Quality Circles, it is a powerful way of identifying possible problems and solutions.

The session explains and gives examples of the different types of thinking – analytical and creative – and then leads into brainstorming as a creative technique. The rules of brainstorming are:

(a) There should be no criticism.
(b) Freewheeling is encouraged.
(c) Quantity of ideas, not quality, is the first requirement.
(d) Everything should be written down, however apparently impractical.
(e) All ideas should be 'incubated' rather than rejected out of hand.

Having introduced the rules of brainstorming, the lesson goes through a seven-stage procedure for running a brainstorming session.

*Lesson plan*
1 Introduce the technique of brainstorming as one of the most important for Quality Circles to master, and ensure that the group knows where to find the relevant material in its books.

151

2   Go through the lesson on brainstorming as outlined in Session 3 of the training manual. When the tape is finished, instead of the real-life brainstorming session which would be used with the Quality Circle, it is best to take a fun subject such as, 'What are all the different ways we can use a Wellington boot?', or 'What are all the ways we could use the resources that the company has now?' The potential leaders on the course will have the opportunity to brainstorm their real problems as a part of a major exercise on the second day of the course, so this will be a useful and enjoyable introduction. Allow ten minutes at the end of the hour allocated to this session to review the material.

3   In the last ten minutes discuss the contents of the tape briefly, and then focus on the mechanics of running the session and ensuring that everything can be completed within an hour. Reinforce the importance, wherever possible, of being able to get an actual brainstorming session into the meeting in which the subject is taught.

### Session 9 – Analysing problems – ninety minutes

*Background*

This tape covers two recommended procedures for analysing problems. This subject is the most complex of those handled, and care is needed to ensure that potential leaders understand the methods well enough to use them.

The first technique is 'Cause and Effect' diagrams, otherwise known as 'Fishbone' diagrams. This is a way of separating causes from effects using the principles of brainstorming, to ensure that the effect being considered is viewed from all sides and that all possible causes are isolated. It involves analysing the effect under six basic headings, which form the basic ribs of the fishbone. The 'cause' categories are people, environment, methods, plant, equipment and materials. These spell out the useful mnemonic PEMPEM. Having introduced the technique, the tape goes on to detail the six steps in constructing a cause and effect diagram.

The second analytical tool introduced by this tape is one called the 'Six Honest Serving-men' or 'Six-word' diagram. This method invites the Circle to explore both the problem and the 'not problem' by using the key words, who, what why, where, when and how. The strength of this method of analysis lies in its insistence on exploring where the problem is not, as well as where it is. For instance, the question 'When does this problem happen?' is followed by 'When does this problem *not* happen?', and similarly for each of the other five words. The technique looks at the balance of pressures of the causes and the 'not causes' as a tool for locating the key difficulties. As with cause and effect diagrams, a six-stage procedure is detailed for completing a six-word diagram.

*Lesson plan*

1  In introducing the session say that two analytical methods are involved and that it is intended to give the group the chance to have a go at each. Ensure the group knows where to find the text of the tape in its books.

2  Using the instructions in the lesson plan of Session 4 in the training manual, play the first part of the tape on 'Analysing problems' as indicated: this completes the training in cause and effect diagrams. Do not wind the tape forward, as the second half will also be used.

3  State that it is intended to try to construct a cause and effect diagram. Because the potential leaders are likely to come from different parts of the business, it is often better in this 'dry run' to choose a more general effect than would normally be the case, so that everyone can contribute easily. Effects like 'poor quality', 'low sales levels', 'failure to meet production targets' can be

153

useful in these circumstances. It should be made clear, however, why such a broad effect has been chosen to work on. About ten minutes should be allocated for the actual construction of the diagram.

4   Thirty to thirty-five minutes should have elapsed at this stage, and ten to fifteen minutes should be allocated for a general review of the technique, the material and the likely best ways of putting over the material to Circle members.

5   After about forty-five minutes of the session have elapsed, attention should be turned to the second technique, six-word diagrams.

6   The instructions in the lesson plan of Session 4 of the training manual should continue to be followed right through to the end.

7   In introducing the fact that the group will work on an example to practise the technique, repeat the point about using a general problem. A different but equally general problem should be used this time.

8   At least twenty-five minutes need to be allocated to constructing a six-word diagram, and this will only allow up to two minutes per question; so time is tight and needs to be managed carefully.

9   Having constructed the diagram, or at least enough of it to have got a feel for the technique, the group should be invited to review the technique, the treatment of it, and the extent to which it seems appropriate to the kinds of problem faced by the company.

### Session 10 – Collecting data – sixty minutes

*Background*
One of the changes encouraged by Quality Circles is the change from an opinion-based way of tackling problems to a more data-based approach, and to accomplish this

successfully the Circles need to become proficient at devising and using check sheets of different types. This training session concentrates on four different types of check sheet, which are suitable in different circumstances. The situations covered include:

(a) Where there is a need to find out how often a range of events occurs in a given period of time.
(b) Where it is necessary to evaluate both the incidence and cost of something.
(c) Where the requirement is to collect information about how long an event lasts and why.
(d) Where the need is to gather data about workflow.

Check sheets are a relatively simple tool to understand conceptually, but great care needs to be taken in designing and using them. These aspects are covered in the training module.

This session is one which has been prepared by a syndicate. Such is the importance of the topic that the trainer needs to be especially careful in reviewing the session, to ensure that everyone has got to grips with it.

*Lesson plan*
1 Introduce the syndicate and invite its members to set up the room as they wish and to deliver the training session.
2 During the session make notes about specific examples of good teaching practice, and also anything that was not handled so well, which may need analysing later.
3 After the lesson, congratulate the syndicate group. Review the lesson in discussion with the whole group, in terms of teaching methods used, the material, visual aids and the importance of the subject. During this review, feed back examples of good teaching which were noted down during the lesson.

155

## Session 11 – Presenting to management – sixty minutes

*Background*

Management presentations are the Circle's opportunity to demonstrate the effectiveness of its way of working, as well as the method of getting authorisation for its main projects. For most members – indeed, for most supervisors as well – presentations will be something outside their present experience. It is likely, therefore, to be threatening to some. It is, however, very necessary that the Circle is competent in presenting its findings, since management will be basing many of its impressions on what it sees during these events.

Technically there is nothing complex about presentations; it is really a matter of understanding the dynamics of such situations, on the one hand, and of having followed a sensible, logical course in the preparation phase, on the other. There are, though, many 'tricks of the trade' which seem obvious but which are in fact the culmination of much experience. These points form the basis of this lesson, which splits up into three broad stages:

(a) preparation for the meeting;
(b) the meeting itself;
(c) follow-up after the meeting.

For the preparation phase the group is given a logical sequence of points to cover, including training in both the importance of, and how to calculate, cost/benefit ratios. For the meeting itself a recommended structure is given, as is advice on the dynamics likely to affect the meeting. In the section on follow-up the Circle is reminded that a 'yes' decision at the meeting does not mean that a magic wand has been waved and that suddenly the action has been taken. The session also covers the very important subject of how the Circle should react in the event of a negative decision by management.

This is the final topic to be covered by a syndicate. During the preparation phase the trainer should have ensured that the members of the syndicate have thoroughly understood the concept of the payback period, and should have advised them to spend time making sure that the rest of the group understands it as well, in the context of both tangible and intangible benefits.

*Lesson plan*
1   Introduce the session as the final one to be handled by a syndicate. Invite its members to set up the room and deliver the lesson.
2   During the session, as before, make notes of specific examples of good teaching practice for feedback later. Take special note of the effectiveness of teaching about payback periods. If some listeners appear not to understand it, decide whether to go through it again as a part of this session, or, if there are just one or two individuals, whether to take them through it separately after the course.
3   After the lesson, congratulate the syndicate and give specific examples of good teaching. Invite the rest of the group to add their comments.
4   Review the material itself. Stress that one of the important benefits of this material is that everyone can follow the text in their own books as it is happening. In addition, they can come back to it whenever they like if they have not understood a part of any particular lesson.

## Session 12 – Working in groups – ninety minutes

### Background
Having a problem-solving structure to work to, and a knowledge of various problem-solving techniques, is only half the battle of working as an effective group. In

fact, it could be argued that most problems faced by groups occur despite their apparent competence to deal with them. The training session on this subject consists of an introduction to the other dimension of group working, that of group process or group dynamics. Groups that are not in control of the process of their work are inherently weak, and run great risks of either failing or at least not achieving their full potential.

Most people have considerable experience of group working and have plenty of knowledge about the subject, though it is usually in the back of their minds, lying dormant. It is recommended, therefore, that this session be treated differently from those that have gone before, and that participants are invited to 'pull' their knowledge about group working to the front of their heads before hearing the tape.

*Lesson plan*
1 Introduce the subject as 'Working together'. State that we all have much experience of working in groups in and out of work, and we probably have experience of groups that have worked well and those that have not.
2 Ask for examples of groups from inside work or outside that have worked better than might have been expected, and those that have done worse. Sports teams are often fertile ground for this discussion, as are various types of committee.
3 State that, in an attempt to record the accumulated knowledge of the participants about the key points of group working, they should divide into syndicates of four to six people each and spend twenty minutes making an organised list in answer to the question, 'What are the things that affect how well a group works together?' Ask participants not to look at their books while doing this, as the idea is to compare notes afterwards. Suggest that a good way of tackling the

task might be to brainstorm the subject for up to ten minutes, and then to arrange the list under sensible headings in the remaining time. Remind the group of the rule in brainstorming that apparently way-out ideas should be encouraged, as well as more conventional ones. Send the syndicates to their syndicate rooms, having asked them to be back in twenty minutes with their lists on flip chart paper.

4    On their return, post the lists up in the room so that everyone can see them. Ask each syndicate in turn to spend a few minutes explaining how it arrived at its list and the reasoning behind it. Make observations about the similarities and/or differences between the lists. Be on the lookout for the 'task' element in the lists, and the 'process' element.

5    Suggest to the group that the tape on the subject of 'Working together' be played now, to give a basis for comparison with the lists that participants have produced. State that the tape will be played and stopped in line with the recommended lesson plan for the session.

6    Go through the lesson plan recommended in Session 7 of the training manual. Try to ensure that the potential leaders grasp the concept of group process.

7    Compare the points made in the tape with the lists made by members by ticking off the ones contained in both. If the syndicate lists contain points about group process, highlight these and congratulate the group. It is likely that these lists will be more extensive, and this is good. Make the point that the tape brings out some fundamental points and that Circle leaders will add to these on the basis of their knowledge.

8    Review the taped material and visual aids. Discuss with the group when the training session should be given to Circles. This decision is important, and the group should think about it seriously.

## Session 13 – Dealing with problems in the group – forty-five minutes

### Background

Groups of whatever type, and whatever intrinsic ability, can have internal or external problems. Faced with such difficulties, the mettle of the group will be determined by its willingness and ability to face such problems and to solve them. No one wants a group to have problems, and it is earnestly hoped that this training session will not be used very often. We would, however, not be fulfilling our obligations were we to ignore the requirement for training in handling such situations.

Since this session would only be used when a need arose, and the present group should not, therefore, qualify, it is recommended that the tape be played through to familiarise everyone with the contents. The stop points for discussion should not be used in this instance.

### Lesson plan

1 Introduce the subject, and the need for it, by pointing out how any group, however good and successful, can have problems from time to time. Stress the point that good groups solve their difficulties; they do not give in.
2 Make the point that, it is hoped, the present group is not in need of this training session, but that it is important to run through it so that everyone knows what it contains, and can have the chance to discuss it.
3 Play the tape straight through.
4 Discuss the content of the tape and the visual aids, and then get participants' views about when the tape should be used – early or late in the development of a problem situation.
5 Close this session by stating that it is hoped no one will have to use this tape.

### Session 14 – Preparation – at least four hours

*Background*
During this session the group, in syndicates of four to six, will be asked to use the techniques which have been covered to identify, analyse, and solve a real problem, and to prepare and give a management presentation of their recommendations to one or more senior managers, who will attend the course for this purpose. The managers' attendance will have to be arranged in advance.

Clearly there will not be enough time for the syndicates to tackle this task fully; data collection, for example, is likely to be a difficulty. A syndicate may, therefore, outline the data required to solve the problem. The purposes of this session are to have participants tackling real problems, and to help them see the methods as a whole rather than as a series of individual and separate techniques.

*Lesson plan*
1   Explain the purpose of this session as being to prepare a management presentation lasting twenty to thirty minutes on real problems faced by the group. To arrive at the presentation, the Quality Circle problem-solving techniques should be used as far as possible, since this will give the group practice in using them with real problems and will help everyone to see them within the whole problem-solving structure. Tell the group which senior managers will attend the presentations.
2   Divide the group into syndicates of four to six people each and say that each syndicate will prepare a presentation.
3   Explain to the group that four hours (more if possible) have been allocated for preparation, and that the facilitator(s) will be available to help if necessary. Say

161

that everyone in the syndicate should play an active part in the presentation.

4   To help organise the time suggest the following time-table (adjusted if more than four hours are available):

| Action | Time (*in minutes*) |
|---|---:|
| Decide on a 'Circle' leader | 5 |
| Brainstorm 'In how many ways can the performance of supervision in the company be improved?' | 15 |
| Incubate the list | 5 |
| Decide the theme and the problem to be worked on, using the Pareto principle | 10 |
| Construct a cause and effect or six-word diagram for the problem chosen | 20 |
| Incubate the diagram | 5 |
| Analyse the diagram by means of the Pareto principle | 20 |
| Decide what facts are needed and what are readily available | 15 |
| Collect facts if available, or list facts required and how they should be collected | 20 |
| Interpret available facts, or estimate facts which will emerge. If the latter, make the point that facts are needed to decide anything | 20 |
| Define solution | 30 |
| Draw up outline of management presentation and decide roles | 15 |
| Prepare presentation | 30 |
| Rehearse | 30 |
| Total | 240 |

Have the recommended timetable available as a handout to the group. Explain that it is simply a suggestion, and if a syndicate wants to organise itself differently, that is perfectly acceptable.

5  During the preparation phase, the facilitators should stay with the syndicate to which they are allocated, and the trainer should have a 'roving brief'. It is obviously vital that the presentations go well, and this means that the trainer needs to spend time in the syndicate rooms ensuring that the preparation time is being used effectively. It is all too easy to spend too long on one aspect of the task, so that time runs out before the presentation has been prepared.

### Session 15 – *The presentations – up to sixty minutes per syndicate*

*Background*
These presentations are important from two points of view. They will represent the first tangible output of the Quality Circle programme as far as the senior managers who attend are concerned. Since first impressions tend to be disproportionately important, the presentations have a key role in establishing the effectiveness of the concept from the start. Secondly, from the point of view of the potential leaders, the reaction of the senior managers is likely to be interpreted as symptomatic of managerial attitudes in general. At the start of any Quality Circle programme the prevailing obsession of supervisors and Circle members is usually with the question of management commitment, so the reaction of the senior people present is just as vital as the presentations themselves.

The trainer, therefore, must not only ensure that the appropriate senior people attend the presentations, but also make certain they understand the two-way nature of the communication. The role of those attending should be to listen to the presentation, to be actively supportive,

163

to ask positive questions, to give whatever answers and commitments are possible, and to do whatever they say they will do by way of follow-up. There is no pressure to make promises. There *is* a requirement to explain to everyone's satisfaction the background and reasons why; and, if action is promised, to 'deliver the goods' within the time specified.

These sessions are usually very productive and positive as two-way communication devices, and are often felt to be the highlight of the course by those attending. Furthermore, quite often positive action comes out of the presentations, which sets the whole programme off on a good footing.

If administratively possible, it is a good idea to organise a course lunch on the last day and to invite senior managers to attend.

*Lesson plan*
1  Introduce the senior managers to the group and explain the outline of the session. The plan is that the first syndicate makes its presentation, followed by feedback from one or all of the senior people, leading into questions and discussions; other syndicates can join in this stage if they want to. The presentation and discussion can last up to an hour. The pattern is then repeated for each syndicate. At the end the senior managers will give general feedback about the session and about their perception of the role of Quality Circles in helping the company.
2  Go through the cycle of presentation and discussion followed by closing statements from senior managers. At the end of the session the senior people should leave.
3  The session should be reviewed briefly in terms of the feelings of participants after their presentations, and their views about the problem-solving techniques now that they have used them.

## Session 16 – *Planning the programme – up to sixty minutes*

*Background*

This session represents the culmination of the course, since, during it, participants will be invited to volunteer to form a Quality Circle, and decisions will be made about the areas in which they should be started. Since more people will have been trained than Circles are to be started, there is a possibility that 'too many' of the supervisors will volunteer. If this happens, the situation must be handled with tact and sensitivity, since the last thing that is wanted is for anyone to feel rejected. The group itself should decide where Circles should be formed if it is a matter of choice. Thought should have been given before the course to the possibility of getting more than enough volunteers, and a decision made about whether, in the event, to increase the number of Circles from the outset or to stick to the planned number. It is often sensible to find out beforehand how many volunteers there are likely to be, since this allows the session to be planned appropriately.

*Lesson plan*

1  Inform the group that the time has now come to decide where to start Circles, and that this obviously depends on who volunteers. Remind the group that participants only volunteered to come on the course, and that now is the time to see who wants to volunteer to start a group. Before volunteers are called for, however, explain that if there are too many, it will be up to the whole group, including facilitator(s) and trainer, to make the decisions. This attitude will ensure that the whole group 'owns' the outcome.
2  Ask for volunteers to start a Circle.
3  If there are too many, make the point that we are talking about phase one, and that in three to four months' time it is likely that more Circles will be

formed. Establish, therefore, that it is not a matter of whether or not to start a group, it is more a matter of when. Suggest that the group brainstorms the criteria which should be used in deciding the areas to start up in.

4   Hold a mini-brainstorming session, writing up the criteria on the flip chart.

5   Agree the main criteria with the group and come to a view with the group about the areas for phase one. Ensure that those not included understand that they will form phase two in three to four months, and that they will all be included in any communication meetings held in the meantime.

6   Introduce the idea of finding an active role for those not in phase one. They could act as deputy Circle leaders, assist with the co-ordination, or perform any other useful roles depending on the particular situation.

7   Decide with the whole group when the first leader communication meeting should be held, usually four to six weeks later, and establish that everyone is invited.

8   Bring the course to a close with a critique. Thank everyone for attending.

# Chapter 10

# MANAGEMENT AND QUALITY CIRCLES

If Quality Circles are to integrate themselves into the normal procedure of a company, there is no doubt that, ultimately, line management must perceive them in a positive light and support them actively. Earning this support is the task of every participant in the programme, especially the co-ordinator. The initial reaction of managers to the idea of Quality Circles, and the proposal to introduce it into the company, is often interesting, revealing, and, at first glance, paradoxical.

Let us consider what the approach offers the line manager. It is saying that staff in his department will be given the chance to solve their own problems, and that they will be trained to do this properly. The fact that people will be doing this will inevitably save a certain amount of managerial time, previously spent trying to solve these same problems, and will enable the manager to concentrate on his own tasks. Furthermore, Quality Circles will improve the performance of the department in a number of ways, including cost reduction and better quality of output. Such a group in the department will materially assist communications between different levels, and can help to reduce and ultimately eradicate any feeling of 'us and them', thereby making for a more satisfying, more successful working life for everyone.

Faced with this glowing prospect, some managers initially reject the concept or remain sceptical about it. The paradox is easy to understand, although care is needed to resolve it. Management has for years been bombarded with new techniques which have claimed to be the answer to every problem, and yet have been found wanting. In consequence, some managers' reactions to any new method will be to say, 'It will fizzle out in a few months' or 'We've seen it all before and it doesn't work'. Their reaction is not only predictable, it is understandable, and says more about the past history of those concerned than about the virtues or otherwise of the technique under review. This does not make it any the less of a problem, but it does change the nature of the difficulty.

A second range of possible reasons for some managers' antipathy concerns the possibility that Quality Circles can be perceived as a threat to the manager. The feeling of threat is most likely to affect managers lacking in confidence, although such a lack of confidence may not be readily apparent. The root of the fear is that the Circles may expose deficiencies and generally 'show up' the manager, and it is no answer to explain that the groups are not there for that purpose, and that a fundamental principle of Quality Circles is to avoid such win/lose behaviour. There is no single solution to this difficulty, rather a range of actions which will ultimately build a situation wherein managers find it easy to support both the concept and the actual presence of Circles in their department.

Making Circles a normal part of the way things are done must be the objective, and the approach cannot really be said to be secure in any area until this is the case, and until the manager actively encourages the groups in his department not only to continue but also to develop their skills further. Then the manager will really be 'getting things done through people', and the staff will have the opportunity to contribute the full extent of their experience and knowledge, should they so wish. The rest of this chapter describes some ways of facilitating this process.

## Induction

All managers will have attended the introductory talks about Quality Circles, and will have, therefore, a basic appreciation of what the approach is trying to do. There is a further requirement, however, which is to give the managers of departments where Circles are to be started the opportunity of learning more about the concept and how it works. The opportunity to attend this session should also be extended to management generally, since it might be instrumental in helping some to come off the fence and support the approach. In larger companies this might entail running more than one session.

The meeting should be scheduled to last for two hours. Its basic objectives are, firstly, giving managers a fuller understanding of the problem structure and the techniques that Circles will be trained in; secondly, clarifying the details of the approach, including the core principles; thirdly, expanding on the details of the plan for the introduction in the company; and, fourthly, outlining the role of management in the programme and answering any questions and worries that anyone might have.

The problem structure and training techniques should be tackled in two ways. Firstly, the training material should be introduced and managers should be given a copy of the members' handbook, to peruse at their leisure. Then the tape on problem-solving should be played through to give the managers a chance to get a feel of how the package actually works. It is often very useful to play one of the tapes which deals with a technique – 'Analysing problems' and 'Collecting data' are recommended. Listening to a tape will give those present a solid induction into the way Quality Circles are developed in terms of their technical problem-solving skills, and will serve to remove much of the mystery about how this is achieved.

The next part of the meeting should review the important principles underlying the concept, and set out the anticipated framework of the introductory programme. The review of the key principles is important, since there is a responsibility for ensuring that the principles are held to, a responsibility which extends to everyone who has any contact with the programme. If the managers can reinforce the key principles from their perspective, and the Circle leader and members from theirs, the approach will bed itself into the normal running of the department or section more easily, and the full benefits will therefore be quicker in coming.

Finally, in the meeting, there should be a discussion about the role of management in the programme. The precise subjects which need to be covered will vary with the company and the prevailing attitudes of the managers concerned, but they should probably include most of those noted below. Firstly, there is the question of what management can do to develop a win/win environment, and how it should respond to the Circles' attempts to do the same. Secondly, there is usually a need to discuss the way in which management should treat the Circles, a subject sometimes much more difficult than it sounds, especially in areas where the introduction of a group significantly changes the way things have been done in the section. Management, for example, can quite legitimately be concerned about how to react to a Circle's performance, notably when the performance has been mediocre. On the one hand, criticism may destroy the group's motivation, and, on the other, praise may give it false hopes. Facilitative skills are required in this situation, and if it is raised as a major worry, either initially or later in the programme, a meeting should be arranged to tackle it, and the sections on group process and review meetings (see pp. 119–28 and 131–9) should be used as the basis for discussion.

A third issue which usually needs tackling is management's attitude to the problems the Circles choose to consider. Some will be minor issues, others will be more significant; some would have been solved anyway at some time, and others may not even have been apparent to management. It is important for managers not to feel defensive about the problems selected; indeed, they should actively encourage Circles to tackle significant problems, since this ultimately will lead to the manager having more time to concentrate on his own problems, thus improving the effectiveness of the department and the organisation. The fact that Circles tackle problems which could or would have been handled by management is actually a great benefit for the enlightened manager, not only in terms of the development of subordinates' skills, and the opportunity for staff to take greater responsibility, but also in terms of being able to get more done with the limited resources of the department.

## Follow-up meetings

The induction meeting is only a start. It is obviously important that this initiative is followed up periodically with review meetings to talk through any prevailing issues. These meetings need only be short, say half an hour, but they are necessary in order to clear everyone's minds, and so that the managers have a forum in which to discuss the programme and what needs to be done. The meetings should be held each month for the first few months, and then whenever the situation demands. There will come a time when these meetings become redundant, that is, when the Circles in the departments of the managers concerned are fully integrated into company procedure. It is likely, however, that managers

171

of departments where Circles start up in subsequent phases will require the same process, and, therefore, it should be accepted that the group is a flexible one, with people joining in as Circles start in their area, and dropping out when all the relevant issues have been settled and Circles are well and truly established in their department.

## Making it easy for management

Circles themselves have a central role in helping their managers to commit themselves fully to the concept. Whatever the attitude of management at the start, approval can become disapproval just the same as disapproval can be changed to approval. The training that Circles receive stresses the benefits of creating a win/win atmosphere, but inevitably there will be difficulties in achieving this all the time in all cases. An important task of the facilitator and co-ordinator is to be sensitive, even hyper-sensitive, to this problem, and the efforts made to overcome it.

One thing Circles must do is to ensure that their manager receives the action minutes of each meeting, so that he is kept fully in the picture as to what the group is doing and how it is getting on. Very often a suggestion by the manager, on the basis of the minutes he has received, either saves the Circle time or helps to give the group a different perspective on a problem. Alternatively, the knowledge of the problem under review has sometimes enabled management to avoid duplication of effort where the particular subject was about to be tackled by another person or group. Another thing Circles should do is invite the manager along to the first ten minutes or so of every fourth or fifth meeting, so that all parties have the chance to ask questions, review progress and generally make sure that there are no misconceptions or difficulties arising out of the work of the group or anyone's behaviour. A third requirement is the more general one of awareness of the need for the group to make it easy for the manager to 'buy in'. Most Circles want management to commit itself to the approach, and to maintain its commitment. The requirement, therefore, needs to be in the back of our mind constantly. After a short time, however, the whole process is likely to become a natural way of doing things, even if it is not so at the start.

## Let the Circles do the selling

Inevitably at the start some people will actively support the idea of Circles, some will actively oppose it, and some will place themselves in the middle. The process of introducing the concept enables those who are keen from the beginning to start up groups, and, progressively, to encourage others, who were not altogether convinced at the beginning, to start up Circles in subsequent phases.

The process of 'converting' people who were previously sceptical is an important one, since they form the basis of future stages. And it is the Circles themselves that are usually in the best position to 'sell' the concept to others, be they managers, supervisors or staff. The best way of doing this is to talk to people about the approach, what it involves and how it works. Talking to people about the approach and how it works will not be of any use, however, unless the Circles achieve demonstrable results. Nothing succeeds like success.

There is also a role for committed managers and supervisors to play in 'spreading the gospel', and this task will be made much easier if the Circles have achieved sound results, and have coped with such difficulties as making it easy for their manager to commit himself, and avoiding any kind of 'élitism'. Circles cannot succeed without management support, because it is only if management agrees that the groups can implement any of their ideas. In the long run it is impossible for such a

**173**

group to exist if the structure above it is not really prepared for it to do so. At the beginning a certain amount of
scepticism from all parties is understandable and acceptable; and at the beginning the programme is an experiment, a time for finding out. Generally the experiment is
successful, in terms of the functioning of Circles, the
relationships between different people and levels, and
the running of the side of the business of which the group
forms part. This fact is a tribute to both the Quality Circle
leaders and members, and their managers.

## Part III
# WILL IT WORK FOR ME?

**Chapter 11**

# QUALITY CIRCLES IN ACTION

The decision whether or not to adopt Quality Circles deserves careful thought. Most of the questions will no doubt be about the concept itself – the extent to which the philosophy, for example, fits in with the way the company is managed or will be managed in the future. There are likely to be doubts about the possibility of operating the approach in certain environments. In fact, Quality Circles are universally applicable. This chapter contains examples of Circles programmes in a wide range of industries, and highlights how different problems relating to the nature or history of the business in question have been overcome. It then outlines a number of individual case histories so as to give a flavour of the kind of situation in which Circles are set up and succeed.

## Electronics/components manufacture and allied industries
Industries such as these are in many ways the natural home of the Quality Circle approach. There are relatively few problems associated with introducing the concept, and the benefits achieved can be very great, since scrap rates tend to be high and expensive. The question often raised in relation to many companies in such industries is whether Circles will work in an environment where many employees are part-timers.

It is often assumed that part-timers, usually women, work for pin money and the chance to socialise, and are totally uninterested, therefore, in anything more than a mundane job. While there may be some foundation to the belief, there is still the question whether the effect is caused by the environment, including the opportunities available, or whether it expresses a genuine lack of interest in anything beyond the routine task. The most likely answer is that there are people in both camps; but there is certainly no problem in getting volunteers who are both willing and able to take part in solving the problems of their workplace. In many instances the Circles formed with such people produce results above average, because the level of ability is often very high among part-timers.

The difficulty which is raised occasionally about the excessive time taken up by a Circle of part-timers is usually a red herring. The point is that Circles are an investment that is invariably cost-effective. Where companies have committed themselves to the idea, they have found no difficulty in justifying it.

One further question, which is sometimes raised, relates especially to industries where technology is both complex and fast-changing. Will groups be capable of contributing in such environments, where possibly only two or three people in the whole business fully understand what is being produced? The answer to this question is usually to look at things like quality reports and scrap rates, and to listen to managers, supervisors and staff talking about what is needed in the business. It is rarely just 'a new product'.

## Heavy engineering, shipbuilding and other large-scale 'production line' industries

These industries often have a history of difficult industrial relations, alienation of the workforce, and general complexity (for example, in shift patterns). Nevertheless, some of the biggest success stories of Circles have come from such environments, often because the need is greater and the approach offers workers a line of communication with management to get things done. This is not to say, however, that there are not difficulties.

Shift patterns can make it hard to arrange meetings where the leader or the Circle members rotate in a different sequence. In one company the men rotated either through two or three shifts, depending on whether they chose to work at night; there was only an occasional requirement for night-shift working; and the supervisors rotated on the same system as the men but in the opposite direction. A more difficult situation for the operation of Quality Circles could hardly have been invented. The 'natural work group' rule had to be broken, because the work group was simply a large number of men with a number of supervisors. Nevertheless, the groups which were formed worked well and produced excellent results.

A problem of when to meet often crops up in such industries. It is usually best for the group, the leader and facilitator to decide this between them. Circles are invariably concerned about lost output, so that there is no danger of groups choosing to meet at times when output is affected more than necessary. Occasionally it will not be possible to meet during normal working time – production lines sometimes prevent it. Where this is the case, the meetings should be held in overtime. Experience shows that this does not result in everyone wanting to join the group just for the extra hour's pay, or in accusations of unfairness of any sort.

Complex union situations and difficult industrial relations are often raised as potential problems in such industries. In fact, though obviously there are difficulties, it is very rare indeed to find that there is not a willingness among enough people, whether they be union officials, managers or workers, to get a programme off the ground. Occasionally Quality Circles will become entangled in management/union issues, but this is rare. Sometimes individual stewards recommend to their members that Quality Circles are to be avoided, and where this is the case, it is vital that the view is respected and that the principles of voluntariness and win/win are adhered to in both spirit and practice. For every steward who responds in this way there are almost always two or three, or more, who are either very supportive or at least prepared to try out the idea for a few months to see what happens.

## Banks, insurance companies, and other 'office-based' industries

There is a popular misconception that Quality Circles are only applicable in production areas. In fact, it has been demonstrated on many occasions that they are just as successful in a wide range of 'office-based' industries. The range of problems to be worked on is just as broad, the opportunities for improvement are just as great, and there are probably fewer impediments to successful Circles than in any others. Indeed, only one is really worthy of mention – the occasional difficulty faced by supervisors who have small sections. Clearly there can be too few people to form a Circle, although there have certainly been successful groups with as few as four members, including the leader. This problem can sometimes be compounded by the need for some people to be 'looking after the office' while the group is meeting. Again there is no doubt that the Circles members themselves are the appropriate people to solve such difficulties, with the aid of the facilitator, if needed.

## Retailing

The retailing industry in the past has had a reputation for managing in either a very paternalistic or a very autocratic way, both of which would be out of keeping with the style likely to bring the best out of Circles. Much of the industry has developed, or is in the process of developing, styles which are more likely to bring the best out of staff, and Quality Circles fit in very well as a part of this process. Against the background of the tight controls needed to run a retailing business, and the increasing standardisation within retail chains, it is sometimes asked whether staff can have much effect, 'as long as they keep the shelves full'. Again, experience shows clearly that staff in retailing units of greatly varying sizes can have a quite remarkable effect on the key dimensions of retailing, based on the knowledge of the  trading figures for their store, and the opportunity to meet and get the best out of their section and solve their problems.

When to meet is a problem in retailing, together with the facts that staff numbers in the different sections tend to be small, and there are often a large number of part-time employees. It is again true to say that the Circles members are in the best position to solve these problems, which they usually do by arranging cover for their section and holding their meetings in the light trading periods. The frequently heard charge that women part-timers are uninterested is usually even less true in  retailing, where, as housewives, they have a keen interest in the whole business from the point of view of the customer, and often put forward excellent ideas for improvements.

One other problem in this industry relates to introducing the Quality Circle concept in geographically far-flung shops. This problem can be handled readily and inexpensively by means of the training package and the members' handbooks, backed up by volunteer facilitators and leaders who can be trained centrally.

## Process industry

It has sometimes been assumed that if there was one industry in which Quality Circles could not work, and would be irrelevant anyway, it was the process industry. Of course, there are very different kinds of 'continuous' process – for instance, cement manufacture is a far cry in many ways from the manufacture of bulk chemicals – and it may be that there are some types of process in which Quality Circles are less appropriate than in others. There are, however, a good many examples of the approach working very successfully in industries as diverse as fine chemicals and steel, so that any assumptions should be carefully thought through and checked out.

The main problems raised concerning Quality Circles in process environments are the difficulty of meeting when the process must go on under supervision, and the complexities of size, alienation and difficult industrial relations referred to earlier in the discussion of heavy industry. The answers are much the same, as well as the questions, as far as when to meet is concerned. Circles settle this in these circumstances in a number of ways, often by arranging for someone in the Circle to cover for them for the duration of the meeting. Such arrangements, of course, have to be made on an ad hoc basis, and occasionally members will be unable to attend meetings because they have been unsuccessful in finding someone to cover for them. When this happens, the leader of the Circle makes sure that whoever had to miss the meeting is brought up to date. It is perhaps interesting that, of all the reasons for members missing Circle meetings, by far the most common are 'pressure of work', and, 'didn't feel he could spare himself from the section'. These reasons say much for the level of commitment of many staff, and are a very powerful argument for giving people the opportunity to contribute through the mechanism of Quality Circles.

This brief discussion of the applicability of Quality Circles in a number of industrial, commercial and service settings has dealt with the main problems on the basis of experience, not theory. One of the most impressive features of Quality Circles is their applicability to any industry if they are introduced flexibly and allowed to fit the shape of the organisation concerned.

# Case histories

### *Cleaners*

A group of cleaners working in the shipbuilding industry were frustrated at the waste they saw all around them. It was their job to clean the ships, to gather waste and dispose of it. They were prone to argue among themselves the case for selling, or giving, this scrap to staff since it was often the kind that would not only be useful for anyone interested in DIY but also would be expensive to buy.

When they set up their Circle, the initial brainstorming session showed them the scale of the problem of waste. Indeed when they decided to tackle it as their first task, many people took the view that it was impossible and that it was something that had to be lived with in their industry. The members of the group were undeterred, however, although they did recognise the need to break the problem down into more manageable parts. They started by collecting all the waste off the ships and putting it into containers. After two weeks they used one of their Circle meetings to analyse the contents and to construct a Pareto chart. This enabled the group to decide that it would focus initially on the waste of nuts and bolts. A further data collection phase in which all the waste nuts and bolts were collected enabled the group to define the size of this part of the problem. They were able to identify the opportunity for saving over £25,000 a year on these items alone. Their solution to the problem was to recommend the purchase of a £200 shed to be sited on the quay and fitted out with racks for different sizes of nuts and bolts. The cleaners were to recycle the nuts and bolts into the shed and fitters were encouraged to go to the shed before requisitioning, to see if any of the right sized nuts and bolts were there. The solution worked splendidly, demonstrating that even 'impossible' problems can sometimes be solved.

### Bottle inspectors

A group of women in the pharmaceutical industry had the task of inspecting full bottles of a particular solution to check that it contained no foreign bodies. Some of their frustrations stemmed from the fact that when the machines broke down they were split up and sent off to do other, usually unproductive, tasks in other sections. The group was also conscious of the fact that the machines broke down frequently and that much production was therefore lost. In the past they had complained about being split up, but their protests had always fallen on deaf ears.

As a Circle they collected data about the performance of their machines and devised a solution based on hand inspection of the bottles when the machines broke down. This had the dual advantage of maintaining production of a much needed product, and also keeping the group together when it would otherwise have been split up. Management accepted the proposal since the cost was minimal, involving the making of some hand inspection booths, whereas the benefits were calculated as being over £400,000 per annum in increased contribution.

This Circle continued its good work by assisting management in the design of a new work area that was being built. Previously the new work area had been the subject of much bad feeling and controversy, but much of the difficulty subsided when those who would be working in the section were allowed to influence the detail of how work would be organised there. Indeed, other supervisors were encouraged to start up their own Circles, and did so.

### Warehousemen

A group working in a large food supermarket identified one of its main problems as being the fact that they did not have time to keep the shelves fully stocked especially at busy times. Their reaction in the past had always been to claim that more staff were needed, but management's reaction had always been that the staffing levels were correct. After forming a Circle, they constructed a cause and effect diagram to try and analyse this problem. This revealed other possible explanations for the difficulty, and the group decided to conduct a detailed investigation into the layout of the shop's warehouse. Their investigation showed that the layout of the shelving was causing congestion. They drew up an alternative layout which would make the whole warehouse much easier to work and managed to sell the idea to the shop manager, even though he had been responsible for the initial design. The Circle took on the job of planning and implementing the changeover with the manager's permission, and this went smoothly as they were able to get most of the other staff in the store to help.

In working the new system they found that not only did they have time to keep the shop's shelves fully stocked, but breakages in the warehouse were significantly reduced, because the whole system was easier to work and less cluttered.

### Order processors

Morale and productivity were at a low ebb when the Quality Circle concept was introduced into the order processing department of a mail order book-selling company. The supervisor decided to try to start a Circle and was successful in getting some support from his staff. The first few problems they tackled involved relatively trivial points such as the location of the rest area, and the provision of screens to prevent draughts. After about three months, however, the group became concerned with the fact that the work area was in a muddled state, with piles of books everywhere. This was a cause of low productivity although the group members were initially more concerned with damage to the books and their own working conditions. Their analysis of the situation showed that they were being seriously hindered by the fact that they worked at simple trestle tables. This meant that books had to be stacked on the floor because they tended to fall off the tables as they were being processed in bulk. They spent a considerable amount of time analysing what was needed, and ultimately designed a new type of desk which would enable them to work more easily and effectively.

To help them sell their solution to management they calculated the effect that the new desks would have on productivity as being about 10 per cent. They also pointed to the improvement in general housekeeping and a reduction in damage to books. Management accepted the solution and authorised the manufacture of a small number of desks to test the effect. Within a very few weeks, it authorised the new desks for all order processors. Productivity increased by 30 per cent, the general appearance of the whole work area was transformed, damage reduced considerably and morale was boosted.

### Makers up

A Circle in the making up department of a hosiery company selected the problem of legs of tights falling on the floor as one of its first projects. The data collected by the group showed that some 750 dozen legs fell on the floor each week. The importance of this related to the loss of value of the products because the fall damaged them, causing them to be downgraded. The Circle's calculations indicated that the cost of downgrading was about £4,000 per annum. In investigating the problem in depth the group constructed a cause and effect diagram which helped to focus on the cause of the problem and the area where it was particularly acute.

The problem was brainstormed by the Circle and members decided on a three-part solution to present to management. These were: firstly, to fit aprons to the machines to catch tights as they fell; secondly, to fit a foam strip to the work benches to increase friction and thus prevent the legs falling off; and thirdly, to fit a protective lining in the boxes under the tables to prevent damage to the tights which did fall.

Management enthusiastically welcomed the ideas and agreed to their introduction initially on a pilot basis, and then throughout the department.

### Paint sprayers

This group in the automobile industry chose as its initial task the problem of vehicles being painted the wrong colour. Over 1 per cent of cabs suffered this fate and the cost of recycling, rubbing down and re-spraying was substantial. The Circle constructed a cause and effect diagram and from this isolated the dual problems of a marking system which could be improved and an attitude problem among certain of their colleagues. Whereas it was management that authorised and introduced the system changes that the Circle suggested, it was the influence of the group on other members of the section which was the real basis of the successful reduction of the problem. By virtue of the informal discussions that the Circle members took it upon themselves to conduct with their colleagues, the problem virtually disappeared and savings of over £3,000 per annum were achieved.

### Pilot scale testers

A Circle in the pilot scale section of a company producing fine chemicals isolated its major problem as that of impurities in the various different batches. This was a long standing problem, indeed something of an 'old chestnut' in the industry, and no one gave the group much hope of producing any solutions of real value. The group recognised that the nature of the problem was such that a long and careful look into the circumstances was required, rather than an instantaneous response. Systematically, therefore, and over a period of months, the group dissected the problem and worked on a range of possible solutions. Ultimately the group decided to put their findings together in a presentation. The basis of their recommendations was so impressive to local management that the Circle was asked to take on the task of contributing to a major programme of capital expenditure in their section lasting over a period of years.

There have been thousands of problems and opportunities which have been tackled by Quality Circles in many different industries, countries and situations. The few examples that we have described show that Quality Circles will work over a wide spectrum of types of group, both skilled and unskilled, and in industries as diverse as supermarket retailing and shipbuilding.

**Chapter 12**

# PROBLEMS AND ISSUES

In the previous chapter examples were given of some of the different types of industry that have adopted Quality Circles, and some of the problems which needed to be overcome in order to help the approach to succeed in these very different environments. Here it is intended to focus on some of the more general problems that can occur with a Quality Circle programme in any industry, and also some of the things that are definitely not problems, despite the worry sometimes expressed about them by senior managers thinking of introducing the approach.

It has been stressed time and time again that Quality Circles do not provide a magic wand, a panacea to make the world perfect overnight. The QC programme is a practical instrument of enormous power if handled sensibly and with sensitivity. One must, however, be able to work through some potential difficulties, none of which are in any way destructive if the real commitment is present, but all of which deserve mention.

## Commitment

The single biggest worry that potential leaders and members express about Quality Circles concerns their perception of the commitment of management to the programme. Commitment from senior management is vital (see Chapter 5), but in a sense it is even more important that the commitment is perceived to be present by employees lower down the organisation. It is relatively easy for management to claim commitment, and to point to such evidence as authorising the programme in the first place, paying for the materials and consultant fees where relevant, and allowing the groups the hour a week to meet.

Such acts do, of course, indicate commitment, but often this is not enough. It is not that supervisors and staff are behaving churlishly in worrying about the extent of the commitment – rather it is a function of their being very highly motivated to succeed and wanting not to put themselves in a position whereby they risk failure because the programme fizzles out. In fact, no special 'rituals' are required to demonstrate management's commitment. Understanding of the needs of participants in the programme is usually enough to remind senior managers to respond appropriately – not in a formal, stiff way, but merely as a normal part of the way they do things.

Clearly, overt commitment is vital at the beginning, for all the reasons stated. It all becomes vital again later in the programme when the first flush of enthusiasm may have died down, and the existing groups have established a routine. This can happen at any time between nine and eighteen months into the programme, and sensitivity from management is needed to judge when a new wave of overt commitment is required. Of course, commitment should not lapse in the meantime; a 'relaunch', however, will often prove beneficial to the programme.

Often this 'relaunch' can coincide with wider publication of the results of the programme, and, in general, a more 'bullish' approach. Many companies have introduced Quality Circle newsletters to act as vehicles for widespread dissemination of the results, and for encouraging more staff and supervisors to volunteer to start groups, and such publicity can help to reinforce commitment to the programme.

The commitment of middle management is another facet of this important subject (see Chapter 10). Wholehearted commitment from middle management is not necessary at the start of the programme, and in many environments a degree of scepticism in the beginning is very understandable. Ultimately, however, line management above the Circles needs to see them as being congruent with, indeed a fundamental part of, its management style.

## Saying 'no'

A worry which affects management mainly, but staff and supervisors to a certain degree, concerns what will happen if management turns down the proposals put forward by the groups. In many ways it tends to be a 'non-problem' in practice, but since it concerns people at the outset, it is important to deal with it. The worry is, of course, that the Circles will become so frustrated and disappointed at management rejecting their proposals that they will give up. The fear tends to be unjustified in a number of ways. Firstly, there is sometimes an assumption that the proposals put forward by the groups will cost massive amounts of money and bring little gain. In fact, because the Circles concentrate on solving their own problems, their proposals do not often cost a great deal, although the benefits are sometimes immense. Secondly, since the groups are trained to understand and use cost/benefit ratios and payback periods, it is highly unlikely that they would put forward expensive proposals not estimated to yield worthwhile benefits. Thirdly, Circles are trained in the importance of living in the real world and very quickly mature in this respect. They are well aware that if they are to get any proposals accepted, they must put up well argued and beneficial proposals, and, furthermore, they recognise that, with the best will in the world, they are unlikely to succeed on all occasions. There will be situations when, however good a case is presented, it has to be rejected for certain reasons.

There are only two things which could cause real difficulties. The first is if the answer was always 'no'. If this were the case, it would suggest either that the groups had not been trained properly in the skills required for effective problem-solving, or that something very strange was happening within management. The second aspect that could cause serious problems is management saying 'no' with no explanation of the reasons why. The guiding principle here is that if the Circle has spent time and effort on trying to solve a problem, the least it has a right to expect is an explanation of why its proposed solution cannot be accepted.

As can be seen, neither of these worries should present many difficulties, and in practice Circle proposals are generally accepted, since they are usually sensible, low-cost answers to problems on which Circle members are the experts. It is understandable that the question of rejection should be raised, and it would be most unfortunate if a Quality Circle programme were to founder because of such a problem. Experience shows that it does not happen.

## Problems disappearing

A problem which sometimes occurs in the early days of a Circle programme is that the groups become frustrated because no sooner do they seem to identify and start work on a problem than it 'disappears'. This is an important phenomenon and must be watched for very carefully. It is usually caused by one of three things. Firstly, it could be that, quite genuinely, the problem was being worked on at the time the Circle identified and chose it. If this is the case, it indicates that communication between line management and the group is not as good as it should be, and the facilitator and leader should review what should have been done to prevent the situation arising.

The second possible explanation is that line management feels uneasy about the group and a little threatened by it. In a situation like this the manager could be saying to himself, 'If I let this group solve a problem, it will show me up as being incompetent; everyone will ask why it wasn't solved before. You can't leave staff to solve problems, that's management's job. I'd better get something done about it straight away'. Of course, such a response might be subconscious and possibly only a part of it would be felt; but in situations like this urgent action is needed, since it indicates that the manager does not see the benefits of Circles to him in his job, and not enough has been done to make it easy for him to support the approach.

The third possible explanation is that the Circle and the manager are playing some sort of 'us and them' win/lose game, and again this needs to be diagnosed and treated quickly. The causes are likely to be either that the manager has a fundamental objection to having a Circle in his department, in which case the inviolable law of voluntariness has been broken – there should not be a Circle in that area – or that not enough work has been done in helping the manager to accept and support the group.

## The style of the business

The Quality Circle approach enables people to use more of their abilities to solve work problems. It presupposes that people have abilities to use. But if the organisation manages its staff in a way which indicates that it does not hold to this belief, Quality Circles would have no place in it.

Undoubtedly there have been, and will be, companies who use Quality Circles as a gimmick, to generate immediate tangible benefits through a manipulation of the workforce. In such companies Quality Circles cannot, and will not, last. It is only to be hoped that such programmes collapse before they disappoint too many people, and before they tarnish the good name of the approach.

Having dealt with some of the main potential problems, we must now deal with some issues which are often raised as possible difficulties but which, in fact, are not.

## Running out of ideas to work on

There are three reasons why this is not a problem. The first is that Circles in their initial brainstorming session generate, on average, about sixty ideas to work on – more than enough to keep them going for some while. There is likely, however, to come a point when the next problem on the list is not very compelling and the ones after it are less so. At this point the Circle can, if it chooses, start to work on opportunities rather than problems. For example, it could say, 'Let us increase our already satisfactory rate of yield from 89 to 94 per cent'. Working on such projects often gives Circles a new lease of life, and is the second reason why running out of ideas is not a problem. The third is that, once the group has developed in maturity and is prepared to accept that it solves its own part of a problem, rather than blaming it all on someone else, it is in a position to start working with other Circles on 'interface' problems. With these possibilities Circles can go on for ever, helping to make things better for themselves, other sections and the company as a whole.

## Disrupting 'production'

The potential of disruption to the work of the section is often raised. Clearly there is a cost in terms of lost output associated with Circles. Indeed, it is 'given' that this will be the case, and if management is not prepared to pay that price in return for the benefits, then it should not introduce the idea. However, the point at issue is often not only that production will be lost for the hour of the meeting but that a significantly greater amount will be lost through the group choosing to meet at times convenient to themselves rather than the best time as far as output is concerned. Quite simply this does not happen. In fact, Circles are usually more rigorous about avoiding lost output than their managers would be if they were choosing the time of the meeting. A point which has been made before and is worth repeating is that the main reason for members missing Circle meetings is that they feel they cannot be spared from their job at that particular time.

## Coming along for the ride

'They'll all just come along for the ride, just to avoid working for an hour.' It is difficult to know when this view is put forward whether to encourage whoever said it to start Circles to learn the error of his views, or whether to recommend that he simply forgets about this approach and continues pursuing whatever style and philosophy he espouses at the moment. Quite simply people do not come along for the ride. This is not to say that it has never happened, it must have done, but it is a tiny fraction of Quality Circle members who are there for this reason. If it applied to a large number, the groups would not last for more than a month, because the members would be so fed up and bored they would go back to work to find something interesting to do! Most people who join Circles do so because they want to get things done. A few might see it as a soft option at the start, but soon learn that it has its own rigours. Of these, a high proportion choose to commit themselves to the group in a full sense, and the few that do not tend to stop coming as they see that the rest of the members are concerned with achievement, not just sitting around doing nothing.

## Calibre of supervision

The low calibre of supervision has occasionally been put forward as a reason for not starting Circles. 'They would never be able to handle the groups', is the usual way of expressing this fear. Quality Circles do not assume that all supervisors are built in the mould of Alexander the Great or Winston Churchill! This is the reason why so much back-up resource is put behind programmes when they are introduced properly. Training material, courses and facilitator help are all designed to help the Circles to become self-sufficient under the leadership of the supervisor. Quality Circles are successful, in the vast majority of cases, not only because the material, training and facilitation are good, but also because most supervisors can be developed to become perfectly adequate, often excellent, Circle leaders and supervisors. Indeed, one of the benefits of the approach is improvement in the calibre of supervision.

## Calibre of Circle members

'You must be joking if you think you'll teach my people stuff like that!' Many potential Circle members will have left school as early as possible after undistinguished academic careers; they will not have seen a classroom for many years and probably will never want to again. But the calibre of Circle members is no more an impediment to learning the problem-solving techniques, and putting them into practice, than it is with supervision.

It would, clearly, be absurd to put over the training material as if it were being delivered to a group of professors, and for the members' handbook to be written in unintelligible academic language. It is, quite sensibly, written in simple English and the great majority of Circle members understand it perfectly well; after all, the concepts are in many ways only rather more formalised ways of describing what everyone does in their lives anyway. The interesting thing about the training of Circle members is that for many of them it represents one of the most important benefits of joining the programme; it is 'gobbled up' hungrily, the handbooks are read avidly, and the lessons are put to use outside the Circle at work, and outside work at home. There is no problem; they are adults, they can cope.

## The trade unions

One potential problem that is almost always mentioned concerns the trade unions. Before this is discussed, however, it is important to note that in the meetings with unions during the first stage of the introduction of programmes, management is invariably mentioned as a key potential problem. There are two ends of every stick!

The TUC has gone into print on the subject of Quality Circles and has expressed a worry, not about the approach in its pure form, but about abuses of the sort discussed earlier in this book. Such worries are entirely natural. In the training given to Circle members it is recommended that, if they are concerned about the motivation of their company, they ask questions about it and expect answers before committing themselves to the approach. Such actions will act as a safety net of sorts. They will not affect the plans of companies who want genuine Quality Circles, but may thwart some of those whose motives are not so pure.

Within companies most are at least prepared to give the approach a chance, and many not only support it fully but are active members of Circles in their own area. The reasons for the extent of the active support given to Quality Circle programmes by stewards is that the concept demonstrates the kind of participation that can be readily identified with. Research has shown that over 90 per cent of stewards favour the idea of participation, and Quality Circles provide an ideal framework for making this goal a reality. They force no one, they enable everyone to take part, they provide the tools to do the job, and they get things done. It is no real wonder that they are supported by positive thinking people, whether they be managers, union officials or staff.

This chapter has concentrated on possible problems which could affect Quality Circle programmes and on 'theoretical' problems which, in practice, do not usually pose any difficulty. It is important to recognise that Quality Circles bring up a large number of very complex issues. There are difficulties associated with introducing them, some 'standard' and others varying with the industry or the precise nature of the company in question. None of these problems is insurmountable, given sufficient knowledge and experience; indeed, the solution to some of them can sometimes ultimately be seen to have been crucial to the long-term success of a programme.

# EPILOGUE

The purpose of this book has been to introduce the idea of Quality Circles and to describe the important aspects of the approach and how to implement it. This last part has concentrated on a discussion of different situations in which the approach has been used, and on possible problems, to enable an assessment to be made as to whether the concept is likely to work in particular situations. The general conclusion, from which it is difficult to escape, is that it is a universal approach. This might at first seem remarkable for a theory which has its origins in the Orient, but, as has been stressed, the approach has its roots largely in the West. Quality Circles have been proved to work in every continent of the world and in virtually every type of industry. If you want them to, they will work for you.

One of the problems which is often raised is that 'now' is the wrong time. 'We've just had redundancies', 'We've undergone a major reorganisation', 'Volume is down', 'We're just coming into our annual wage negotiation', say the pessimists. There is no ideal time to do anything, as is testified by the grey hairs on the heads of senior executives everywhere! It is important to establish as far as Quality Circles are concerned, though, that there really is no 'right' time except now. Quality Circles have been introduced just before, just after, and even during redundancies; while business has been good and while business has been terrible; and before reorganisations, during them and as a consequence of them. The point about the Quality Circle is that it is a device for enabling people to contribute by using their abilities to help make things better. Things can always be made better, and there are always enough people who would like to be given the chance to help.

A part of the decision whether or not to introduce the concept should be an assessment of the potential benefits. To make sense, this should be done with the specific business in mind. It will be as well, therefore, to review what is the present state of the company in terms of its 'style', the performance of supervision, the attitudes and performance of the shop floor, communications, and possibilities for tangible improvement in quality and performance, which could all be influenced by Quality Circles. After current performance has been reviewed along these lines, the next step is to establish what situation represents the desired future state. If there are substantial differences between the present and the desired states, Quality Circles may well be worth introducing.

Quality Circles are deceptively simple. They have far more to them than is at first apparent. The in-company Quality Circle programme, of which this book forms the first part, provides all the material needed to introduce a programme, as long as the training and facilitative skills are available in the company, and as long as there is access to resources who have experience of Circles in practice.

Do it, but do it properly, because it is worth doing properly.

# INDEX

# INDEX